Praise for

FARMING, FOR REAL ESTATE AGENTS

"Meredith Fogle has written a must-read guide for any agent ready to transform their career by developing a geographic real estate farm. This book guides the reader step by step through the journey of identifying, cultivating, and dominating a real estate farm. Follow her systems and get ready to take your business to the next level!"

—David Parker, Esq., President, Village Settlements, Inc.

"Meredith's book provides a simple, clear, and actionable approach to agents as they look to learn and explore geographic real estate farming. By using the step-by-step instructions and worksheets included in the book, readers can walk away with a business plan ready to execute."

—Kimberly Gladis, Author, *Leading Teams*

"If you have the will, this is the way. This book is not about theories, it is a plan that has been tested and refined. Reading this book will take care of one of the fundamental stages of growing a business: having a plan."

—Chad Older, JD, MBA

"Having established herself as one of the most successful real estate agents in the Kentlands/Lakelands communities, Meredith Fogle is highly qualified to provide insight and advice to her peers on how to transform their careers via an effective lead-generation system, which will in turn yield return, repeat, and referral business."

—Gina Dropik, Editor, *Lakelands Leader* Newspaper; Director of Communications and Administration, Lakelands Community Association

"After working with Meredith numerous times on real estate transactions, I can say that she is the consummate professional! After reading this book, not only is my initial opinion true, but her real estate acumen has far exceeded my expectations! Read the book. It will not disappoint!"

—Chong Yi, Producing Branch Manager, The Yi Team Mortgage

"Meredith Fogle, an altruistic realtor who has risen to success unselfishly, shares her secrets with the world through her book, *Farming, for Real Estate Agents.* Meredith learned from her mentor, Judy Howlin, how to methodically grow a successful business by focusing on being honest, ethical, and knowledgeable with everyone she encounters (future buyer, seller, or just a friendly neighbor). Having lived on Meredith's 'Farm' for the past 19 years, I have seen firsthand her progression to become a top realtor."

—John K. Bucy, Entrepreneur, Staffing Executive

"Meredith has written a delightful, must-read guide full of important information for anyone considering real estate farming . . . Read this book—and learn from one of the best and most well-respected agents."

—**Sean Sheppard,** Business Development Manager, TruPlace

"Meredith Fogle has written a must-read guide for any agent ready to transform their career by developing a geographic real estate farm. As a broker, I have tracked Meredith's success for years. I have always been impressed by her constant ability to dominate her farm year after year. Now you have the ability to learn her and other successful agents' farming secrets."

—**Chris McMahon,** CRB, Old Line Properties, LLC

How to Cultivate a Real Estate Farm
and Transform Your Business

FARMING,

for

REAL ESTATE

AGENTS

Plus secrets of top-producing famous farmers

MEREDITH FOGLE

RIVER GROVE
BOOKS

Published by River Grove Books
Austin, TX
www.rivergrovebooks.com

Distributed by River Grove Books

Design and composition by Greenleaf Book Group
Cover design by Greenleaf Book Group

Publisher's Cataloging-in-Publication data is available.

Print ISBN: 978-1-63299-333-5

eBook ISBN: 978-1-63299-334-2

First Edition

*Dedicated to Judy Howlin, mentor extraordinaire
and Kentlands' first famous farmer*

CONTENTS

PREFACE

RESIDENTIAL REAL ESTATE is a highly competitive field in which success can be elusive. One of the first things I tell people who are interested in becoming agents is that good agents make it look easy. Most real estate agents continually strive to find consistent success and reliable income, but the vast majority flounder and fail. My goal in writing this book was to provide a quick, effective, and focused path to success for potential, new, and struggling real estate agents. I want to help you make more income with less effort. And I want to help you create instant differentiation among the vast field of your competitors.

I have been harnessing the power of real estate farming for over 20 years, and have used it to build an award-winning career. I work in one of the most sought-after areas of the Washington, DC, suburbs, where I live and have built strong relationships with the community, purposely building my reputation and brand as the Kentlands real estate expert in Gaithersburg, Maryland.

Relationship building and being visible and active in the community are crucial components of growing your market share. As my own team grew, increasing the efficiency with which my business runs through the use of systems has also been key; having effective, replicable, delegable systems in place for lead generation, lead management and follow-up, listing management, and transaction management is vital. Those systems have allowed me to run the most successful local real estate business in my area while also remaining involved in other activities and staying engaged with my family.

Real estate farming is the business strategy that has allowed me to build relationships and to ensure visibility and community involvement. It has given me a distinct edge over my competition, integral market expertise, and an immediate bond to my client base. My farming success is the result of my ability to articulate my passion for the community in which I live and my ability to invest in and build relationships with farm-area residents. I often say that I do almost as much to sell the neighborhood as I do to sell the listings I market.

Real connections are the key to success. Although affiliating with tech-first brokerages may seem like an easy way to impress leads, tech-first brand strategies may actually prevent you from creating the local connections that are the beating heart of a successful real estate business. They can also be risky to your career: one major company recently reduced its agent count by half due to falling revenue, and another delayed its planned public offering due to lagging growth and falling market share. Technology gives us some great tools, but those tools can never replace the value of personal connections. These tech-heavy companies are failing. To combat this failure, agents are returning to the grass roots of real estate: relationships.

The more global communication becomes, the more important local expertise becomes. The real estate agent who becomes the local expert has provable value over the incoming discount- and tech-brokerage competition, as well as the competition from the next town over. Local expertise also provides potential clients with the knowledge that their agent has the inside track on all things farm-area related, whether that is school information, area amenities, changes to infrastructure, updates to the area's master plan, or plans for a new local restaurant, store, or housing. Farm-area experts also often know about listing inventory not yet on the market and can provide their clients first access to upcoming homes for sale—especially important in a tight market.

By becoming that local expert and by building relationships with the local community, you can give yourself (and more importantly, your clients) the upper hand in the market. You'll have first access to local news, which you can then share with your sphere of influence. Farm-area residents will come to know you as the inside source for local information, and your community connections can be a benefit to you and your clients when an issue arises for which you or they need quick action.

This easy-to-follow guide provides everything you need to know to successfully sow, grow, and harvest an endless stream of prospects from your farm. You'll learn the tools and systems that are key to successful farming and that you can start to apply to your business today. These are the same secrets that made me the most successful agent in my real estate farm, and they can help you dominate your market, too. You'll also hear from rain-makers across the country who share their ideas and the secrets of their success. Simply follow the steps outlined in these pages to learn how to turn your farm into a lucrative business promising steady income and reliable, long-term success—and that may one day become a sellable commodity.

Introduction

WHAT IS A FARM?

DO YOU LOVE the sound of roosters crowing at dawn? The sight of cows methodically chewing their cud? The farm-fresh fragrance of chicken coops? Neither do I. But how about the cha-ching of a check clearing the bank? The smiles of your clients as you hand them the keys to their new home? The sweet smell of success? Those are my favorites, and those are the fruits of a well-run real estate farm!

Like a traditional farm, a real estate farm is a limited geographic area in which you plant seeds, tend your crops, and harvest the fruits of your labor. Your seeds are marketing and lead generation. You'll tend your crops by building and strengthening client relationships, providing exceptional listing and buyer services, and positioning yourself top of mind for buyers, sellers, and referrers in your farm area. Finally, you'll harvest repeat and referral business that results in market dominance over time. You'll harness the power of systems to yield further growth, allowing you to expand and even, one day, to sell your farm.

Some of the wealthiest real estate agents in the business are real estate farmers. Farming works. When run properly, a real estate farm is an easily sustainable, consistent, low-cost source of long-term income. Farming helps focus your business and is by far the most effective way to generate leads and referral business.

Any successful real estate agent knows that the real business of real estate is, at its core, the business of lead generation. A successful agent must be a master lead generator—a rainmaker. The best agents quickly discover that an efficient, prolific, and cost-effective lead-generation system is key. Real estate farms are among the best lead-generation tools. That's why so many of the most successful agents farm for business. A well-run farm provides an endless supply of prospects, yielding eventual return, repeat, and referral business.

Go to **www.therealestaterainmakers.com** to download a free copy of the *Farming, for Real Estate Agents* workbook. Completing the exercises outlined in these pages is essential to your success as a real estate farmer, so you'll want the workbook at your side as you begin this journey to transform your real estate career. Once you've read the book and completed the workbook, revisit the website to unlock other secrets of real estate success, including Farming Systems, downloadable marketing tools, lead conversion success scripts, video training, support, coaching, and much more.

FINDING YOUR FARM

SELECTING A FARM area is both a personal and a professional decision, and it is one you should consider carefully. Once you've selected your farm, you'll be investing time, energy, and money into your chosen farm area. Your decision should be based partly on your familiarity with and the feel for the farm you are considering and partly on numerical data.

Choose with your heart

To be truly successful, you'll need to be involved in and knowledgeable about your farm area. Naturally, it's much easier to be involved and interested in a community you love. You'll be marketing to this area, participating in and sponsoring community events, and working within the community to take listing and buyer meetings and to tend to your crop of listings and buyer sales. Many successful real estate farmers live within their farm areas.

Living outside of the community you farm can make this level of engagement difficult, though not impossible. Some successful real estate agents farm communities in which they have lived previously or in which they someday hope to live. Farming a community similar to that in which you live (another resort community, another historic community, another 55-and-older community, another new urbanist community, or a similar condominium complex) can be effective.

Wherever you choose to farm, be sure you have a passion for your farm area. Clients can sense an agent's level of interest in his or her farm area during the listing or buyer appointment. The passion you bring to your farm can often tip the seller or buyer in favor of working with one agent over another.

Once you begin working in the area you love, you may not want to work anywhere else.

INTERVIEW WITH A FAMOUS FARMER
JUDY HOWLIN

Judy Howlin was Kentlands' first resident realtor and successfully farmed the then-brand-new, new-urbanist Washington, DC, suburban community. Judy served as my mentor, and here she shares insights about how she began farming and how she ultimately dominated her farm area.

What were the most important considerations to you in choosing your farm area?

I chose the community I lived in. It was the area that I knew and liked best.

What were the most important steps you took to secure your position as the top agent in that farm area?

I got to know people in the community in many different ways (other than real estate), all the while letting people know that I was a real estate agent. By being honest, ethical, and knowledgeable in all my interactions with my neighbors and members of the community, I hoped that they would see that I strived for the same in my business. They would get to know me as a responsible, effective person and seek me out when they needed real estate assistance.

Did you face any challenges?

Since it was a very popular and lucrative area, there was a huge amount of (agent) competition. I just had to stay steady and consistent.

What were the most important recurring activities or tasks you included in your business plan to gain market share?

I consistently mailed out original and distinctive post-cards with my photo and house photos, notifying the

continued

community of my sales and listings to keep the community constantly reminded that I was in the real estate business. I also frequently held open houses in the community because I knew many of the people who would tour through. Since there were so many different types of homes in the community, people really liked to tour houses when they were open. I rarely held open houses in other areas. I produced professional-looking color brochures describing features for each home with photos and floor plans.

What aspect of farming a specific geographic area did you find most rewarding?

I loved the people and the homes in the community. Many people moved from house to house within the community. I was able to know almost all of the homes intimately and many of the people personally. I had many multiple transactions with the same people and the same homes. I was able to secure the largest percentage of the business in the community and developed built-in credibility despite the overwhelming amount of (agent) competition.

Choose with your head

Once you've identified an area you love, it's time to do your research. You'll need to analyze sales history data to be sure the prospective farm can support your business goals.

First, use this exercise to find out whether the farm you've identified has enough turnover to make it worthwhile to concentrate most of your business there.

1. Go to your local MLS and run a history of sales in the neighborhood over the past five years.

2. Find the total volume for each of the past five years (listing and sold volume). Use the space below to calculate the volume for each of the last five years for your neighborhood:

   • Year 1 total neighborhood volume: _____

   • Year 2 total neighborhood volume: _____

   • Year 3 total neighborhood volume: _____

   • Year 4 total neighborhood volume: _____

   • Year 5 total neighborhood volume: _____

3. Find the average of all volume results: _____

4. Find 5% of the average volume: _____

5. Multiply the number above by your average commission amount per transaction (remember to subtract any split with your broker): _____

6. Find 10% of the average volume: _____

7. Multiply the number above by your average commission percentage per transaction: _____

8. Find 25% of the average volume: _____

9. Multiply the number above by your average commission percentage per transaction: _____

The results of the calculations in steps 4, 6, and 8 represent your potential income at various percentages of market share. If you were able to secure 5% market share, could you reach a viable income number? What about at 10%? If 5 or 10% market share represents a viable income amount, this is an area that can support your business, and therefore in which it might make sense to farm. 25% market share or higher might represent a five-year goal you can set now.

Take note of the total volume trend as well. Is total home-sale volume increasing year-over-year on average? If so, the time is ripe to jump into this market area.

Vet the competition

Now it's time to examine your potential competition. Is there room in your prospective farm market for a new agent? The lack of more than one consistently dominant farm-area agent may mean there is room for a new agent to capture market share. A single dominant agent might mean some sellers are looking for an option. Inconsistencies in market share can also indicate there is an opportunity. A market wherein many agents each have a relatively small market share indicates a market ripe for an area expert. How can you find out whether an opportunity to seize market share in a farm area exists? Use your local MLS to analyze market share trends by following these steps:

1. Find the total number of transactions in your prospective farm area for the immediate past 12 months.

    Total transactions: _____

2. Identify the top five agents by number of transactions over the past 12 months and the total number of transactions for each of these top five agents.

    Agent 1: _____Number of transactions: _____

    Agent 2: _____Number of transactions: _____

    Agent 3: _____Number of transactions: _____

    Agent 4: _____Number of transactions: _____

    Agent 5: _____Number of transactions: _____

3. Divide the total number of transactions for each agent by the total number of transactions in the farm area for the past 12 months (include both listing side and sell side closed transactions) to calculate each agent's percentage market share.

    Agent A: _____%

    Agent B: _____%

    Agent C: _____%

    Agent D: _____%

    Agent E: _____%

4. Repeat the previous steps for the prior four years to fill in the following chart to examine changing market share over time.

	Year 1	Year 2	Year 3	Year 4	Year 5
Agent A					
Agent B					
Agent C					
Agent D					

Here's how the numbers looked as I took over in my farm area.

	Year 1	Year 2	Year 3	Year 4	Year 5
Agent A	35%	7%	12%	21%	10%
Agent B	23%	15%	10%	12%	13%
Agent C	23%	27%	24%	15%	17%
Agent D	20%	17%	6%	13%	17%
Agent E (me)	4%	15%	22%	24%	30%

As the chart illustrates, I started out with only 4% market share as I began to farm the area. However, my research showed that the agent with the largest market share the year I started farming (Agent A), had an inconsistent market share history. The numbers also indicated the lack of one highly dominant agent and no single agent steadily taking over market share. The door was wide open to secure my spot in the farm area.

By year two, my consistent farming efforts were paying off and my market share tripled. Agent A's roller-coaster trend continued, agent B's share dipped, while agent C saw a market share jump. Agent D's share remained fairly constant.

My market share grew nicely into year three as I continued consistent implementation of my farming systems and remained confident that dedication to a client-focused business would lead to an increasingly strong reputation over time. Agent A's market share continued to wobble. B and C were on a downswing, while D's numbers fell drastically.

Four years into focused work building my real estate farm, my market share exceeded that of the other top four agents. Agent A's share bobbed back up but still remained below my number, while agent B's share remained almost equal to the previous year's number. In an effort to stay a fading presence and to compete with me, agents C and D decided to team up, which turned out to be a fatal mistake.

By my fifth year, my market share stood at a solid 30%, and has grown consistently ever since. Agents B and C eventually gave up and moved out of the neighborhood. Agent A moved her office out of the neighborhood and focused in another area, at which time her market share fell precipitously. Agent D maintains a handful of transactions per year, and his market share continues to diminish. Today, my market share stands at 62%, and has remained between 55% and 62% for the past nine years. Here's a snapshot of the trend as my market share grew over the initial five-year period.

AGENT MARKET SHARE

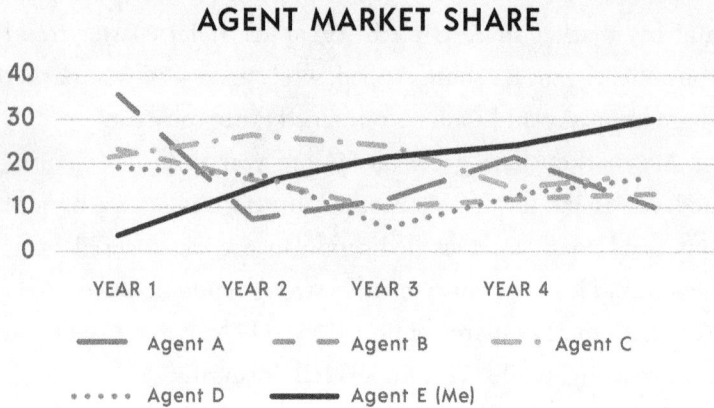

The lesson: focus on your goals and keep your eye on the big picture. Do not allow yourself to become distracted worrying about what the competition is doing; be consistent, and focus on doing the right things, always putting your clients first. The competition will take care of itself.

The result: lead generation becomes easier as more business is referred; prospects begin to call in response to signs, ads, and online marketing; and positive word of mouth spreads. Listing and buyer appointments become less competitive. Agents working with buyers shopping for homes in your farm area contact you to be put on a waiting list for upcoming listings. Frequent buyer leads provide enough business to feed a team of agents. This is the goal of a successfully run real estate farm.

Farming new construction

Why farm a to-be-built neighborhood? Because no other agent has dominated this area. Executed correctly, farming a newly constructed community can be highly lucrative. While the long-term maintenance of a new construction farm is similar to that of a traditional real estate farm, these first steps, unique to new-construction farming, are essential to secure your place as THE agent in a newly built or to-be-built community.

Establish yourself as the go-to agent for information

Find out everything you can about plans for the new community. What housing types are planned? Who are the builders? What are the names of each model? What features make each model different? What are the available options for each model? What are the planned price points? What community amenities are being offered? Is there a retail or commercial element? If so, what companies are planning to lease space? What other features or amenities make the new community special or unique?

Visit the builders early and often

As soon as trailers or construction offices are in place, be one of the first to stop in to visit the on-site sales staff. Take copious notes about what the builders are planning. Collect any floor plans you can get your hands on. Become conversant in the specifics of what makes each builder and each model unique. Find out fun facts about the community: Where did the street names come from? Is the community modeled on any other neighborhoods or concepts? What is the history of the land on which the community is being built? What type of community management or HOA is planned, and what will be included in the HOA fee? What schools are planned for this community?

Let the builders' reps know you are planning to help advertise their new community, and request that the reps inform you about community news or changes. The buyers' agent commission is already built into the pricing for newly constructed homes, so builders' reps are more than willing to keep you informed, especially if they know you'll help them sell their product.

Communicate the information

Spread the word about the new community using every method at your disposal. Create a new community website. Use social media to post about the new community. Create a community blog. Create a neighborhood listserve or newsletter. Use print ads to market yourself as the new community's expert. Send postcards to surrounding neighborhoods and place ads in local newspapers positioning yourself as a resource for information. Let fellow agents know you are a budding expert about the community and share your information freely with those fellow agents. Create a database containing the contact information for anyone who approaches you for information about the new community. Update your database members, your website, your social media, and your blog every time new information about the community is released.

Collect contact information for every resident who moves into the community

Create a database listing the names and addresses of every purchaser and renter who moves in. Update your database monthly with new resident information. Using this information, begin a consistent monthly mail campaign, sending postcards to every community resident. This postcard should list recent neighborhood home sales data, should include a free home value analysis offer, and should feature a call to action to contact the neighborhood real estate expert (you) when a resident of the new community is ready to buy or sell.

Advertise every listing and sale you make in the community through every available outlet

Use every possible marketing method to advertise your community sales. Blanket the neighborhood with directional sale signs placed at every intersection pointing buyers to your neighborhood listings. Place an "I Found the Buyer" sign on the lawns of properties for which you represent buyers. Include photos of your sales and listings in your online, social media, and print marketing.

Consider purchasing in the new community

Is the new community a neighborhood in which you could see yourself living or owning an investment property? Residing or owning in the community gives you an insider's edge.

Don't forget to go to **www.therealestaterainmakers.com** and download a free copy of the *Farming, for Real Estate Agents* workbook to follow along with the exercises.

PREPARING YOUR FARM

THINK OF YOUR farm as a business into which you will invest substantial effort and money over a long period of time. Preparing your farm properly is vital to ensuring the best return on your investment of time and financial resources. Follow the steps in this chapter to lay the groundwork for a fertile farm that produces profits year after year.

Create a business plan

You've probably heard the quote, "A goal without a plan is just a wish." Setting goals and then breaking those goals down into small, accomplishable steps is essential to fulfilling your long-term objective: farm-area dominance. Decades of research proves that creating a set of written goals puts your subconscious mind to work while you take purposeful action to achieve each step. Goals create focus; what you focus on expands. Once you've taken the time to put your goals into writing, you'll begin to notice reminders of those goals all around you as you begin to manifest success.

VISION BOARDING

A vision board can serve as a useful tool to help your subconscious focus on your achievement goals. Studies of successful salespeople show that the best way to achieve results is to utilize both visualization and goal-setting techniques. Exposure to visual images of your goals dramatically increases your ability to achieve those goals. Goal-setters who include visioning in their planning experience a marked increase in their percentage of goals met.

In order to create a vision board, gather a piece of poster board, scissors, glue, and several magazines and/or your computer. Flip through the magazines or surf the internet to find images that embody your goals—not just physical items, but images that give you a feeling of pleasure and well-being. Your vision board should include both things you want and things you want to experience and can include words as well as pictures.

Once you've cut out or printed out the images that represent your goals, affix them to your vision board and display your finished board in a place where you will see it every day. Then let your subconscious do the rest.

Outline your goals

Successful real estate farmers possess a clear sense of purpose. These agents maintain focus on their long-term destination and are master goal-setters. Most agents work to achieve financial goals as well as personal fulfillment.

Let's take a moment to identify what motivates you, the larger reasons you do what you do, and the goals that correlate to those motivators (and for purposes of this exercise, let's assume that personal fulfillment is a given).

What are the three reasons you work (your motivators)? My motivators were my family, my future, and financial stability. Write your three major motivators here.

1. _____

2. _____

3. _____

What are the specific accomplishments you wish to achieve relating to each of these categories? Mine were the ability to send my kids to college without requiring them or us to accrue debt, to plan for a future that would involve plenty of travel and time with my husband, and saving a "nest egg" large enough to ensure future financial stability. Write your three specific accomplishment goals here.

1. _____

2. _____

3. _____

Now, identify an "extra" that would be possible for each of the previous categories if you exceeded your goals. Mine were the possibility of helping my kids with the cost of post-graduate studies (or funds for their first house if they chose to forego graduate school), the possibility of owning a vacation property, and saving enough to allow us to purchase additional investment properties. Write your three "extras" here.

1. _____

2. _____

3. _____

Break down your goals

Now that you've identified your major motivators, articulated your specific accomplishments, and identified the "extras," it's time to break your goals down into concrete steps.[1]

Begin by quantifying the value of each goal (in other words, the actual dollar amounts needed to fulfill each of your specific accomplishments). For example, in order to send each of my three children through college without taking out student loans (and assuming their tuitions were not offset by financial aid or merit awards), I calculated that starting in 2018 I would need to have saved approximately $55K (using the average cost of the schools my son hoped to attend) for each of the following

---

1   This goal-tracking exercise was inspired by and adapted from an exercise in the book *The Millionaire Real Estate Agent* by Gary Keller (New York: McGraw-Hill Education, 2004).

four years. However, I had a second child entering college two years later who was considering similarly priced schools. That meant an additional $55K for four additional years, two of which overlapped my first child's college years. So, in reality I needed to have saved $110K for two years, and $55K for the next two years. Oh, and then there's that pesky third child, still seven years away from entering college. That's an additional $55K per year for four years—but not until seven years down the road.

At first glance this total of $660K seems overwhelming. But remember the saying about the best way to eat an elephant: one bite at a time. Approach goals the same way. When broken down into reasonable "bites," what can appear to be an unreachable goal becomes quite achievable. Let's take my financial goal as an example. In order to send all three kids to school debt-free, I will need to have saved that $660K over a 15-year total time period. That's $55K per year, which doesn't seem quite as overwhelming.

Broken down into transactions per year at my average per-transaction commission rate and average price per transaction, $55K means five additional transactions per year, which seems achievable. Since I have the 15-year total time span to achieve my overall earnings goal, even if I have one stellar year and one year that is less than stellar here and there, the numbers balance out in the end. The key is to keep my focus on my long-term goal.

Breaking this example down even further allows us to identify the number of additional listings and buyer agreements needed to reach the goal number. Using my average conversion rate, this means an additional six listings or buyer agreements per year. Breaking it down further still into the number of additional listing and buyer appointments needed using my average conversion rate, achieving this goal means seven additional listings and buyer appointments per year—very manageable.

Not following? Don't worry. We're about to break down your big goals into year-over-year numbers and to find out exactly how many transactions, listing agreements, buyer agreements, and even appointments you'll need to accomplish your goals.

Choose one of the specific accomplishments from your previous list and calculate the value (how much money you will actually need to achieve your goal). Repeat this exercise for each of the three specific accomplishment goals and enter your numbers below.

Goal 1 value: _____

Goal 2 value: _____

Goal 3 value: _____

Calculate yearly income needed

For each of the accomplishment goals you just listed, calculate the number of years in which you plan to (or need to) complete each goal. Then, divide the value of each goal by the total number of years.

Goal 1 value per year: _____

Goal 2 value per year: _____

Goal 3 value per year: _____

Calculate your goal numbers

The total of these results represents the total gross income you'll need per year to reach your goals. Now that we know that number, it's time to set your specific goals for the first year. Follow the steps and use the following worksheet to calculate exactly how many transactions, agency agreements, appointments, and leads you need to fulfill your yearly goal. I've also included an example worksheet using an annual income goal of $200,000 to help you follow the math.

1. First, enter your annual income goal onto the income goal line on the upcoming worksheet.

2. Now, divide your income goal number by your average commission percentage per transaction (the example uses my personal historical average commission per transaction: 2.5%) to arrive at your volume goal number. Enter that number onto the volume goal line.

3. Next, calculate the number of transactions you'll need to close to reach your volume goal. Divide your volume goal by your historical or projected average transaction amount to find this number. (In the example we use an average transaction amount of $500,000, resulting in a goal of 16 total transactions). Enter your result onto the transactions goal line.

4. Now, use your average historical or projected agreement conversion rate (the percentage of signed listing and buyer agreements that actually result in closed transactions) to find the number of signed listing and

buyer agreements you'll need to reach your transactions goal. Divide your transactions goal number by your average appointment conversion rate (the example uses an average conversion rate of 85%, resulting in a goal result of 18.82; we rounded up to 19). Enter your result onto the signed agreement goal line.

5. Last, use your average historical or projected appointment conversion rate (the percentage of listing and buyer appointments that actually result in signed agreements) to find the total number of listing and buyer appointments you'll need to reach your signed agreement goal. Divide your signed agreement goal number by your average appointment conversion rate to calculate the total appointments you'll need to hit your signed agreement goal (the example again uses an average conversion rate of 85%, resulting in a goal result of 22.35, which we rounded up to 23). Enter your result onto the total appointments goal line.

EXAMPLE INCOME GOALS

Income goal: $200,000

Volume goal: $8,000,000 ($200,000/.025*)

Transactions goal: 16 ($8,000,000/$500,000)

Signed agreement goal: 19 (16/85%)

Appointments goal: 23 (19/85%)

*commissions are always negotiable and vary from market to market

YOUR INCOME GOAL WORKSHEET

Income goal: _____

(your first year annual income goal amount)

Volume goal: _____

(your income goal amount divided by your average commission percentage)

Transactions goal: _____

(your volume goal divided by your average transaction amount)

Signed agreement goal: _____

(your transaction goal divided by your average conversion rate)

Appointments goal: _____

(your signed agreement goal divided by your average conversion rate)

Now that you have your goal numbers, you may want to take the worksheet one step further to calculate the breakdown of listing versus buyer sides. If you are primarily a listing agent and 75% of your transactions are listings, that means you'll need 75% of those transactions to be listings and 25% to be sales, and vice versa.

Track your progress

Now that you have identified the total sales volume and the number of total listings and sales you'll need in order to reach your goals, you can break those numbers down further still into monthly goals. Using a worksheet, which can be as simple as a spreadsheet (see the following for an example), outline your goals per month. Use the spreadsheet to track your progress each month.

At the beginning of every new month, revisit this sheet, entering your actual numbers from the previous month, record the average volume and total volume for that month, and note the outstanding variance. Each month you'll move closer to your goal. If you find you've had an off month and did little or no volume, remember that in real estate some months are naturally busier than others and work to bridge that delta in the coming months. Continuing to track your production will keep you motivated.

Sample goal tracking sheet

Net income listing goal	Goal per month	Jan	Feb	Mar	Apr	May	June	Jul	Aug	Sep	Oct	Nov	Dec	To date actual	Variance
Listing Agreements	10	2													-8
Listings Sold	8	1													-7
Average Price	$500,000	536000													36000
Sold Volume	$4,000,000	536000													-3,464,000

Net income buyer goal	Goal per month	Jan	Feb	Mar	Apr	May	June	Jul	Aug	Sep	Oct	Nov	Dec	To date actual	Variance
Buyer Agreements	9	1													-9
Buyer Sales	8	0													-8
Average Price	$500,000	0													
Sold Volume	$4,000,000	0													-4m

Monitor your production results monthly to stay on track. Your subconscious will work toward your goals, and you'll feel rewarded as you see your measurable results progressing toward your yearly goal each month. Goal setting and monitoring are vital exercises for any agent. The real estate farmer with a laser focus on goal achievement will see increases in farm-area production year over year. You'll also use your year-end results to set new goals as each new year begins.

Your goal-tracking sheet

Net income listing goal	Goal per month	Jan	Feb	Mar	Apr	May	June	Jul	Aug	Sep	Oct	Nov	Dec	To date actual	Variance
Listing Agreements															
Listings Sold															
Average Price															
Sold Volume															

Net income buyer goal	Goal per month	Jan	Feb	Mar	Apr	May	June	Jul	Aug	Sep	Oct	Nov	Dec	To date actual	Variance
Buyer Agreements															
Buyers Sold															
Average Price															
Sold Volume															

Don't forget to go to **www.therealestaterainmakers.com** and download a free copy of the *Farming, for Real Estate Agents* workbook to follow along with the exercises.

3

SOWING THE SEEDS

LET'S REVISIT THE farm analogy. You as an agent are one of thousands of farmers operating one of hundreds of farms across your region. How will people find you? What sets your farm apart? Sure, your produce has to be fresh and attractive. Sure, your farm stand needs to be well marketed and visible to passing traffic. But what will make your customers loyal clients who return to you again and again? What will make your clients send everyone with whom they discuss real estate your way? What will keep people buzzing around your stand while the stands of your competition remain sparsely visited?

Now that you have a clear vision and established goals, it's time to sow the seeds that will result in leads, agreements, and closed transactions. The seeds you plant as you establish your farm are your presence, the fresh approach that differentiates your services, your area expertise, your involvement in your farm area, the relationships you develop, and your personal interactions with farm-area residents, consumers, and fellow professionals on a day-to-day basis. These elements work together to create an indelible impression and to establish the reputation that will serve as the foundation for your thriving real estate farm.

Provide a fresh approach

Even in farms where one or two agents have been historically dominant, a fresh approach can result in quick growth of market share. One way to shake things up is to bring a unique perspective or innovative tool to the market. Many agents use the same sales techniques and marketing strategies year after year, so you'll stand out right away by offering something different. Are you a technology guru? A social media wiz? Do you have a special connection to likely buyers for the farm area? Do you hold a professional designation that makes you unique? Does a cause or charity you support set you apart? Perhaps the fact that you live in your farm area differentiates you. Perhaps you are a native of the region or an alumna of a local school. Make note of what differentiates you, and use your distinctiveness to your advantage.

Create a compelling marketing message

Every communication to your prospective client base must include three elements: your key differentiators, a special offer or compelling reason to contact you, and a call to action or a direct request for business. Let's outline these three elements; they will become the basis for your elevator speech (see the following box) and for all of your farm-area marketing messages.

In the space below, choose a key differentiator that makes you unique and the reason that differentiator appeals to or benefits farm-area residents.

Differentiator: _____

(Example): I'm a resident of this neighborhood. I care as much as you do about property values here and will work harder than any other agent to sell your house for top dollar.

Next, describe the special offer you plan to include as you begin your farm-area marketing efforts. Your special offer might be a limited-time discount for using your services, a free comparative market analysis (CMA), a free staging consultation, or a discount from a member of your vendor network.

Special Offer: _____

(Example): I'm offering free staging to any seller who signs a listing with me by January 31st.

Finally, draft your call to action or direct request for business.

Call to Action: _____

(Example): Call, text, or email me today to take advantage of this special offer.

As your business evolves and you have other differentiators to highlight, such as dominant market share, highest sold volume, lowest days on market, or other successes, be sure to include these new elements to keep your marketing message fresh. We'll revisit these elements in greater depth when we discuss marketing later in these pages.

Now that you have outlined these three elements, you can use them to develop your 30-second "elevator pitch."

THE ELEVATOR PITCH

Using the differentiator, special offer, and call to action you listed previously, create a brief statement to use when anyone asks you about your services. Here's an illustration using the previous example elements.

"It's important to work with an agent who cares as much about your property values as you do. As a resident of this community, there's no one who cares more and who will work harder to sell your house for top dollar. Right now, I'm including free staging for any listing I take before January 31st. Would you like to set an appointment to do the listing paperwork now so you'll be able to take advantage of my offer to stage your house for free?"

Use the following lines to draft your first elevator pitch.

_____

_____

_____

_____

_____

_____

_____

Become the area expert

The most successful farmers position themselves as farm-area experts. Research about your chosen farm area is required for you to attain expertise. Begin by learning the history of the community. Source original newspaper articles, developer information, and builder brochures to find out all you can about the original plan and vision for the community. Follow records back as far as possible to the time the community was an undeveloped tract of land.

Create a timeline illustrating the development of the community, including ownership changes and plans that may have been abandoned or redrafted. Tell the story of the eventual developer's original vision. Did the developer include a mission? Was there a *charette* or other process from which the final plan emerged? Did the final plan divert from the original vision? Were there surprises along the way? What fun facts can you share? Knowledge of the community's unique and special features will help to position you as the expert in the eyes of both farm-area buyers and sellers. The results of your research may serve as content for your website, blog, or for a farm-area-focused brochure or pamphlet you create. The anecdotal history you'll be able to share will both impress future clients and will help build relationships.

Become an expert on every builder who built in the community and be prepared to articulate both strengths and weaknesses. Know each model and every option for each model. Collect floor plans whenever possible and compile them into a database for easy reference. Let residents know that you likely have their floor plan; when a homeowner reaches out to you for their home's floor plan, you'll be one step closer to building a relationship that may result in a future listing.

Become conversant about any issues facing the area or proposed plans for the community. Attend meetings at which information about these issues or plans might be discussed. Talk to community leaders to gather as much factual information as possible. Learn how to handle possible buyer objections to proposed changes and to highlight the benefits of living in your farm area. Be aware of new events in your community such as new festivals, community parties, or other social events, and be prepared to attend and sponsor those events. The more knowledgeable you are, the more you'll be able to intelligently discuss farm-area issues, activities, and changes that may affect your farm area and its property values.

Brand your business

Developing a recognizable brand is essential to cementing your position as the farm-area expert. Your tagline and logo together create your brand, which will then be reinforced by your track record and reputation. To create your tagline, crystallize your key differentiators into a simple phrase that encompasses your intrinsic value and your reputation. Perhaps you are the boutique real estate agent, the agent who specializes in house-to-house moves, the agent who gives back, the online marketing expert, or the neighborhood's resident real estate agent (the tagline I use).

Once you have your tagline in place, create a logo that speaks to your style. Some creative agents choose to originate their own logos, while others hire professionals to create a bespoke logo design. Whichever path you choose, it's important to consider how you want your audience to perceive you. You should include colors that appeal to you and imagery that connects your brand to your chosen farm area. Take a look at some iconic brands' logos and you'll see that they share a few basic qualities: clean lines, printability in color and black-and-white, and the ability to evolve over time (check out the Starbucks logo, one of the world's most recognized logos, as it has evolved over the years)—and all are instantly recognizable.

Your brand should be emblazoned upon every piece of marketing you send and should be included in your online and social media platforms. Your brand encompasses your value and your reputation, which will be called to mind each time a prospective client reads or hears your tagline or sees your logo.

INTERVIEW WITH A FAMOUS FARMER
DEBBIE DRUMMOND

Debbie Drummond brands herself as the Las Vegas Luxury Home Pro. Her intimate knowledge of the Las Vegas market, her branding, and her blogs and monthly newsletter have made her one of Sin City's top producing real estate agents. Here, Debbie describes how branding helped her build her business.

How did you choose your farm area?
It's the area where I live. I moved here in 2005 but

continued

didn't start farming this area until just a few years ago. At first, I wasn't sure I wanted to farm my own neighborhood but now I'm glad I started.

What makes your farm area unique?

Las Vegas tends to have homes that are in subdivisions. My neighborhood is a bit different. It's more custom homes on large lots rather than subdivisions. We even have some horse properties mixed in. The variety of home types and the way custom homes vary from one to the next means that living here gives me a better understanding of the farm market than someone who doesn't live here.

What do you feel has been your most effective marketing tool?

The big thing is to be consistently building your brand. I send lots of postcards with my picture and branding on them, which takes consistency and time. I'm visible at local restaurants, shops, etc. I'm also a CRS (Certified Residential Specialist). Otherwise, my website has been my best marketing tool. That, combined with social media, has exposed (my brand) to many out-of-area clients.

Looking back, is there anything you would have done differently?

I would have started farming my area earlier.

Put up your shingle

Once you start to advertise your first farm-area listing, your most visible shingle will be your yard sign. Until you secure that first listing, you'll need to advertise in other ways to create visibility within your chosen community. Does your community have a neighborhood newspaper or newsletter? If so, purchase ad space in those publications and run an eye-catching ad matching the message included in your postcard campaign. Further increase your presence and recognizability by sponsoring community events. Purchase a large banner featuring your branding and smiling face for use at community activities or sporting events you sponsor. If a banner isn't appropriate, purchase branded signs to post at those events.

Be sure your online presence is excellent as well. Get a website up and running and begin a social media campaign. The more visible you are in as many places as possible, the more you will be top of mind for your potential future clients when they are ready to buy or sell a home. Once you have that first listing, be sure your yard signs include your branding. If you are with a brokerage that requires you to use a brokerage-branded yard sign, consider an eye-catching sign-rider or additional yard sign you can hang alongside your broker's signage. Enhance your print and online marketing with "just-listed" advertising—good for you and great for your new listing.

Go door to door

Now that you have your elevator pitch ready to go, your marketing in place, and a special offer ready to extend, it's time to make a personal connection with your farm-area residents.

The best way to do that? Go door to door during a time you know many of the residents will be home. Many agents choose to make their door-to-door visits on the first warm spring day or a particularly beautiful fall day and often on a weekend to ensure the best possibility of interacting with community residents. Does going door to door make you uncomfortable? Good. Discomfort with an action proven to get results is the number one reason 80% of agents fail to take that action—and why the 20% who are willing to do what's uncomfortable do 80% of the business.

Choose a nice day to make your door-to-door visits and be sure to take something of value with you to give away to the people you meet. Consider creating a door-hanger you can leave if no one is home that includes the three elements of your marketing campaign on one side and a list of recent home sales on the other. Neighbors love to be in the know about their local market so an update about a recently sold neighboring property is an excellent conversation starter if the resident is at home when you visit.

When you do find a resident is home, keep the conversation brief and always ask for business before you leave. Practice introducing yourself using your elevator pitch and thanking the neighbor for taking the time to talk with you. If the resident has no intention of buying or selling in the near future, let him or her know that you often know of buyers in the market for houses like theirs and ask if they know of any neighbors who are planning to sell soon. Chances are they'll point in the direction of a neighbor they've heard may be planning to make a move. When they do, make a note of the address and make that house your next stop.

Get to know farm-area buyers

One way to get to know where your farm area's most likely buyers will come from is to conduct an informal poll to find out where current homeowners lived before moving to your farm area. While you are going door to door or when you are in conversations with farm-area residents, ask those residents how they found out about the community and where they lived before moving to your farm area. This information will give you unique insight into how best to market your future listings and the most effective places to advertise to attract farm-area buyers. Once you have this information, be sure your marketing is positioned to reach those buyers. Target print, online, and social media advertising toward those buyers and the agents most likely to be working with those buyers. Get in touch with relocation companies who may have future buyers for your farm area and arrange to give them early access to or information about upcoming listings in which their relocating employees might be interested.

Compile a list of the agents who have brought two or more buyers to farm-area listings within the past two years and create an e-flyer campaign targeted toward these agents, who might also have other buyers looking in your farm area. Compile a list of top agents who work in other areas outside of your farm area from which farm-area buyers have come. Reach out to those agents; let them know you are the go-to agent for your farm, and offer them a preview of homes coming onto the market that might be right for their buyers. Not only will these methods help your listings sell faster and for top dollar, but they may also help connect you directly with farm-area buyers you'll be able to bring to farm-area listings, further increasing your market share and track record as the top agent in your farm.

Get involved

One of the most important ways to exhibit your intent to commit to your farm area is to get involved in the community. Too many agents spend endless hours learning everything they can about the business of real estate, sitting in a classroom, or behind a computer analyzing sales data. While it's important to spend time learning and staying up to date on market trends, the bread and butter of real estate is personal interaction with potential clients. Real estate rainmakers have a saying, "It's not what you know, it's who you know!"

Not only will your involvement in your community prove personally rewarding, but it will also make you more visible as an active community member. It will help you build relationships with other community members, and will help build trust with farm-area residents—and the more people trust you, the more likely they are to conduct business with you. Remember that in order to benefit, you need to be a benefit; and you'll naturally want to give back to the community that has given you so much.

Begin by contacting the person or organization that plans community activities and ask for a list of events planned for each year, an event the community would like to add, or suggest a new event of your own creation. Choose at least one event to sponsor or to run, and plan to do more than simply donate funds. Always attend the events you sponsor to get to know more people in your farm area. Community is created in part by shared experience, so the more you share, the more a part of the fabric of the community you will become. If you can help create that shared experience, even better.

If your farm area is a new community or a community that

does not host or plan events, become involved in the philanthropic branch of your HOA or community management organization (if one doesn't exist, consider instituting one). Become active in your school PTA (or even better, become a PTA board member or chair school events), or join or initiate a community club or athletic team—find an event or activity that speaks to your passion. As farm residents see you becoming an engaged community member, or better, if they recognize you as a leader (preferably in a non-political sense) capable of running large events or taking on complex community roles, they'll feel even more confident about working with you when it comes time for them to buy or sell one of their largest assets.

Build trust

Real estate is, above all, a business of trust. Your clients will be entrusting you to handle the transfer of one of their largest assets and the asset that is likely closest to their hearts: their homes. Building trust begins with building relationships. The old saying, "People don't care how much you know until they know how much you care" is largely true.

Successful real estate farmers build real relationships first. Many count their clients among their friends and experience significant cross-over between their personal and business lives. Enter every relationship genuinely and never with the goal of transacting business. Demonstrate first and foremost your care and concern for the people in your community and for the greater good of the community, and you'll begin to build trust. In real estate, reputation is everything. Always lead with the intent to serve your community and to help make the lives of the residents of your farm area better—and your business will organically grow. The trust you build through genuine relationships will lead to trust enhanced by a solid track record of closed transactions. That track record will lead to countless referrals, solidifying your market share as you watch your farm grow and flourish.

INTERVIEW WITH A FAMOUS FARMER
AMY BROGHAMER

Amy Broghamer is a top producer in Cincinnati, Ohio, and is the author of the book *The Playbook for Success*. Amy has built a successful team and real estate business largely by building relationships with her clients. She encourages those clients to rely on her team as they would on family to help them through the process of home selling or buying. Here's what Amy has to say about building her business by building trusting relationships.

How did you choose your farm area, and how long did it take you to become the area's dominant agent?

I grew up in northern Kentucky, across the river from my farm area. My hope was to build my business in my current farm area. When I first moved to Anderson Township, it took a little while to dig in and about five years to become dominant.

What specific steps did you take to become the dominant agent?

I concentrated on what I call "relationship farming." My community is family focused, so I got to know the people in the community. I spent my time and money on people who already knew and liked me. I hosted client events and was sure to thank everyone who referred business to me. I do my best to matchmake for my clients. I strongly believe that what is best for my clients is best for my business. Also, I started a Facebook page for Anderson Township where I post local events and activities. I intersperse video, sales stats, and other real estate-specific information in my content. My business is now comprised exclusively of repeat and referred clients.

Is there anything else you've done to help build relationships and trust within your farm area?

Yes, I got involved in the economic development committee, in which no other females were involved at the time. I've been on that committee ever since. I also served on several subcommittees, which made me more visible by serving in a supportive but non-political way. Getting involved in my kids' schools has also been invaluable. I sponsor the preschool open house event and the Halloween coloring contest. I network at sporting events, sponsor my kids' sports teams, and host team parties. I try to be a value-add and at the

continued

same time keep reminding people that I am in the business of selling real estate.

It sounds like you've been very purposeful in the way you've developed your business.

I maintain a very specific set of standards and will turn down business. I have a minimum price range. I've also built a network of agent partners to take referrals for business that is more than 30 minutes away. I use systems to run my business efficiently so I can focus on building relationships. I do try to be very purposeful in every interaction as well as being as personal as possible, focusing on building one-on-one relationships. I believe in the saying, "When you speak to everyone, you speak to no one."

Be a consummate professional

Whether you are starting out in real estate or building your business in a new farm area, your reputation matters. When you exude a professional image, your farm-area residents will think of you in a professional manner. An impeccable reputation and a professional image will go a long way toward opening doors in your new farm. Here are a few rules of thumb to follow.

Dress professionally

In order to establish yourself as a professional in the eyes of your farm community, you'll need to dress that part whether you are running to the grocery store, picking kids up from school, or grabbing coffee or lunch with a friend. Those who don't know what you do for a living will recognize that you are in professional attire and may ask about your business, giving you an opportunity to connect with a potential future client; and those who do know what you do for a living will see that you are always ready for your next appointment.

Keep confidentialities confidential

The fiduciary duty of confidentiality is vitally important, especially when you work in a tight-knit community. Never share information that your clients have not given you explicit and written permission to share. If your standards are above reproach, your stellar reputation will precede you, making buyers, sellers, and other agents more willing to work with you.

Be kind

You've heard the old adage, "If you don't have something nice to say, don't say anything." That saying applies to real estate, too. Speak kindly of others and always treat the public and other real estate professionals the way you would want to be treated. Enter every transaction expecting the best and with an attitude of cooperation and positivity. You'll soon note that the kindness you exude will be returned to you.

Communicate professionally

Keep emotion and personal opinion out of your transactions and communications. Your clientele relies on you to serve as an emotional buffer during what can be a stressful transaction. Always communicate with other agents, lenders, title companies, and their staff with a professional tone and thank them for the work they are doing. Reread texts and emails before hitting send to be sure they convey the message you intend and are free of typos or other errors.

Get to know other farmers

Learning from and building relationships with other real estate farmers may be one of the most valuable activities you'll undertake as you become the area expert for your own farm. Reach out to successful agents who concentrate in geographic farms and offer to take them to coffee or lunch or, if those agents are in other areas of the country, request a phone or video conversation. Using the interviews in these pages as examples, ask other farmers how they broke into their farm areas and what they did to build their businesses. As you speak to these farming success stories and read the interviews contained in this book, you'll gain new ideas and insights to bring to your own farm-area business.

Now, imagine you are the dominant agent in your farm area, and answer all of the questions you've asked the farmers you've interviewed. Then draft a plan for how you will become the dominant agent in your farm.

Don't forget to go to **www.therealestaterainmakers.com** and download a free copy of the *Farming, for Real Estate Agents* workbook to follow along with the exercises.

4

BUDGETING FOR SUCCESS

EVERY GOOD BUSINESS person knows that a well-thought-out budget is essential to running a successful business. That's true with a real estate farm as well. The truism that you have to spend money to make money is valid, but you'll find that the more successful and visible a real estate farmer you become, the more demands will be placed on you financially. As your business grows, you'll be asked to donate to private causes and to sponsor events, you'll need to purchase more business and office supplies, and you'll need to invest in better technology. You may find that you need to hire staff to support your growing business. You may even be enticed by paid lead-generation platforms or fancy CRMs.

Before you know it, you could be spending almost as much money as you are making. That's why a sound financial budget is essential. Equally essential is a carefully planned time budget. While you have to spend money to make money, time is the one commodity that cannot be created, so be sure to spend your time wisely.

Create a financial budget

Your goal should be to keep your total business expenses within 10-15% of your gross income. Let's revisit your goal net income to find your total business-expense budget. Take the goal net income number you identified in chapter 2 and add 10-15% to that number to calculate the gross income you'll need to allow for business expenses. Using the example goal net income of $200,000, adding 10-15% brings your goal gross income to $220,000-$230,000. Using this example, the total business-expense budget should therefore stay within $30,000. The newer you are or the lower your net income, the more difficult it will be to stay within that percentage. However, beginning with a careful budget and consistently monitoring that budget will help to instill the good long-term financial habits you'll rely upon as your business grows.

Setting your budget at the beginning of each year and avoiding sizeable budget deviations during the course of the year can be easier said than done, so you'll have to begin with careful planning. If you are beyond your first year of business, begin by comparing your actual expenses from your previous year to your total commissions earned. Create a chart or spreadsheet (see the following worksheet) that clearly defines expense types and compares your budgeted expenses to your actual expenses. Then, use the spreadsheet or chart to map your planned expenses for the coming year and to make adjustments up or down based on the goals you've set and the commission you realistically think you will earn for the coming year. If you are in your first year in real estate, use the same worksheet and eliminate the "prior year actual" column.

Next, schedule a quarterly budget review of your expenditures, your income, and your planned future expenses for the remainder of the year. A financial accountability partner such as your broker, your spouse, or a colleague can help review these numbers to ensure an objective approach to your budget. That person can also serve as a sounding board to help you evaluate the wisdom of future unplanned expenditures or donation requests that arise throughout the year and that might exceed your planned budget.

Real Estate Budget Worksheet

Expense Type	Prior Year Actual	Expense Type	Current Year Budget	Current Year Actual
Office Supplies		Office Supplies		
Office Space		Office Space		
Website		Website		
Postcards		Postcards		
Brochures		Brochures		
Newspaper Ads		Newspaper Ads		
Other Print Ads		Other Print Ads		
Signage		Signage		
Sponsorships		Sponsorships		
Community Events		Community Events		
Client Parties		Client Parties		
Social Media Ads		Social Media Ads		
Technology		Technology		
Donations/ Volunteering		Donations/ Volunteering		
Education		Education		
Vehicle		Vehicle		
Copies		Copies		
Promotional Items		Promotional Items		
Association Fees		Association Fees		
Other		Other		

Create a donation budget

Every successful and visible business deals with requests for donations or sponsorships that come after a budget is set. As with any unexpected expenditure, these requests require careful consideration; in large or publicly held companies similar requests would require board or member approval. So, what happens when the community in which you farm introduces a new event or opportunity to which it might make sense for you to contribute?

One year I was asked to purchase supplies for my community's 5K race. This race has become a huge local event with thousands of participants, hundreds of volunteers, and receives a fair amount of local media attention. However, the supplies I was asked to provide would have exceeded my budget by almost $2,000.00. Moreover, the request came in during a meeting I attended in August, a full eight months after my budget had been set for that calendar year. Since I tend to adhere closely to my budget, my initial instinct was to decline the request. However, as I sat through the meeting, I ran a simple litmus test composed of a few questions.

First question: Does my recent sales history justify an expenditure increase? My commissions earned for the year so far slightly exceeded my earnings goal to date, and my pending sales were above my goals for the coming few months as well. Answer: Yes.

Second question: Is the expenditure for a good cause? This particular event is the major fundraiser for our Community Foundation, whose mission is to maintain and further the character of our community and the vision of its original founders. Answer: Yes.

Third question: Will I see a return on my investment? This question is always the most difficult to answer. A return can manifest in a number of ways, from increased visibility (as in this case), in the form of leads or referrals (difficult to quantify in this case), or in general goodwill from your farm residents (as in this case). For me, two out of three yeses to this question were equivalent to a solid yes.

Since the request passed my simple litmus test, I decided to approve the request. Try using the same test the next time you are asked for a monetary donation. Sometimes, the only return you'll see on a donation is the personal reward that comes from giving. That in itself can often be enough.

Create a time budget

Your time is by far your most valuable asset and the most limited, so spend it wisely. As your farming efforts result in an increasingly fruitful and growing farm, you'll be tempted to pour more and more time into your business—after all, it's lucrative and it's your passion. However, remember that the busier you become, the more difficult it may become to maintain a healthy work-life balance. As with your financial expenditures, the best way to ensure you are spending your time wisely is to create a sound budget. Use the following steps to get started.

Examine your current time usage

Using a calendar or the following worksheet, record every activity you undertake during each hour of every day (it's best to do this at a relatively busy time so that you have a realistic sense of how many hours you are spending and how you are spending them). Include *every* activity: sleeping, eating, showering, gym time, social time, as well as your work-related activities.

	Mon.	Tues.	Wed.	Thurs.	Fri.	Sat.	Sun.
12 AM–1 AM							
1 AM–2 AM							
2 AM–3 AM							
3 AM–4 AM							
4 AM–5 AM							
5 AM–6 AM							
6 AM–7 AM							
7 AM–8 AM							
8 AM– 9 AM							
9 AM–10 AM							
10 AM–11 AM							
11 AM–12 PM							
12 PM–1 PM							
1 PM–2 PM							
2 PM–3 PM							
3 PM–4 PM							
4 PM–5 PM							
5 PM–6 PM							
6 PM–7 PM							
7 PM–8 PM							
8 PM–9 PM							
9 PM–10 PM							
10 PM–11 PM							
11 PM–12 AM							

Color code:

Now, color code each activity line by line. You can choose any assortment of colors you like, but for the purposes of this exercise, try this breakdown:

- Green for revenue-producing business activities (listing appointments, buyer or showing appointments, writing contracts, presenting offers, attending seminars, holding open houses, networking and other face-to-face meetings, or lead-generating activities with clients or prospects).

- Blue for non-revenue-producing business activities (working on marketing pieces, preparing presentations, completing CMAs, working on your website or social media, furthering your education, coaching, attending office meetings, etc.).

- Yellow for family or social time (meals with family or close friends, helping kids with homework, attending kids' sporting events, visiting with your siblings or parents, having a date night with your spouse or significant other, etc.).

- Purple for miscellaneous activities (vacation time, gym time, salon time, your morning routine, working on a hobby—anything that does not fall neatly into the categories listed above).

- Gray for the hours you sleep.

Assess your time usage

Once you've color-coded your week, you should be able to quickly identify areas in which you may need more balance. First, look specifically at your green and blue areas (your business-related activities). Are you spending more than half of your business time on non-revenue-producing activities? If so, set a goal to shift that balance so that you are spending increasing time on revenue-producing activities. That simple shift will result in more closed business. Next, compare your green and blue areas to your yellow and purple areas. Are you spending more than half of your time in green and blue? If so, you may want to reexamine your work-life balance to be sure you aren't setting yourself up for an unsustainably rigorous work schedule that could lead to burnout.

• • •

You now have all of the essential elements in place to establish a fruitful farm: you've identified a farm area, you've set goals, you've begun to sow the seeds that will lead to a successful harvest of leads, and you've set a solid budget. As you become increasingly successful and your farm begins to grow, remember to consistently review your goals and your budgets to ensure you remain on track and as balanced as possible. Now it's time to take your farm business to the next level.

Don't forget to go to **www.therealestaterainmakers.com** and download a free copy of the *Farming, for Real Estate Agents* workbook to follow along with the exercises.

5

HARVESTING THE FRUITS OF YOUR FIRST LISTING

IF YOU'VE FAITHFULLY followed the previous steps, you probably already have your first farm-area listing or lead. If so, congratulations! If not, revisit the previous steps to ensure you are consistently implementing the strategies suggested until you have that first listing. Once you do, your next step is to harness the almost unlimited lead-generation potential your first listing presents. This first listing will be key in growing your farm-area market share, so it's essential that you effectively market the listing and advertise your success when you get that listing sold.

As a general rule, each listing should spawn at least one new listing and at least three buyer agreements. Follow the steps outlined in this chapter and watch as your first listing snowballs into multiple additional transactions. Continued marketing around every future farm-area listing and sale that results from this very first listing will grow into exponentially more business and, over time, will bring you farm-area dominance.

Hold it open

Open houses can be a great way to sell your own listing. Marketed and conducted effectively, an open house will attract potential buyers who may start out "just looking" but might fall in love when they walk through your listing. Follow these steps to unlock the potential your open house presents.

Market the open house

A well-marketed open house maximizes buyer traffic—good for you and great for your listing. You'll need to do much more than simply post the house as open in your local MLS.

Use a variety of platforms to advertise your open house. Mail or hand-deliver open house postcards or invitations to surrounding homes or to areas in which potential buyers reside. Feature your upcoming open house in your newsletter, splash the open house announcement across your social media platforms, run social media ads, post a rider advertising the open house on the yard sign, and blanket the neighborhood with open house directional arrows 24 hours before your planned open house. Contact local agents to personally invite them to come visit your open house.

Prepare your pitch

In order to sell your listing to the agents and buyers who will visit your open house, you'll need to prepare a brief pitch highlighting the home's assets. Before your open house, memorize all of the listing's special features, the recent upgrades and improvements, and the basic facts and figures (year built, square footage, lot size, etc.), and be prepared to briefly describe those facts and features to every buyer who comes through the door. Be sure you are also ready to articulate the attributes of the listing's location and the local community. There's no better way to demonstrate your expertise than effectively communicating your knowledge of the details of your listing and of the surrounding community.

Build rapport

Welcome every buyer who comes through the door and learn about motivation right away by asking how they found out about the open house. Did the buyer come after viewing the house online or was the buyer sent by his or her agent? If so, this buyer may be a better prospect than the buyer who simply followed your directional arrows, but you won't know until you ask a few questions, some of which you can include in a simple open house sign-in form. Always require that buyers sign in before touring a property. This is vital for safety and security both for you and your sellers' property, and will give you additional information about the buyers' intent and motivation. Sign-in forms will also allow you to collect contact information, vital for follow-up once the open house concludes.

New open house software allows buyers to sign in from their own smartphones, detects bogus email addresses, responds with an auto-email thanking the buyers for visiting and offering further assistance, and even automatically sends the buyers' contact information to you in a CRM-ready format.

Invite the neighbors

Some sellers may be hesitant to allow an open house because their perception is that all of their "nosy neighbors" will come through their house (a perception often perpetuated by agents who don't know how to hold an effective open house or who prefer not to spend their weekends working). However, neighbors can prove a fantastic neighborhood grapevine network marketing tool and should be welcomed. In many neighborhoods, neighbors may also be motivated buyers. Consider inviting neighbors for a "neighbors-only open hour" the hour before the first public open house is scheduled to begin. Not only will this make neighbors feel special and welcome, it may also help keep the real "nosy neighbors" from pulling your attention away from ready buyers during the remaining hours of your open house.

Sell the community

As the farm-area expert, you should be able to articulate the value of living in the community better than any other agent. Consider creating a flyer or brochure that lists community amenities, describes the history of the community, and includes a community map. Not only will this help you sell your listing, but it may also attract future buyers who meet you at the open and recognize you as the farm-area expert. Some of the neighbors who stop by your open house may even be so impressed by your area expertise that you'll be the first agent they call when they are ready to sell their own homes.

Follow-up

Immediate follow-up at the conclusion of your open house is vital. The most effective method for converting an open house visitor into the buyer of your listing or into a buyer who chooses you as their agent is quick contact directly after the open house, when the buyer has just interacted with you while touring your listing. Plan to devote the hour immediately following the open house to follow-up.

Start by reviewing your open house sign-in forms or information and ranking them in order of importance, with buyers who showed interest in the listing at the top and buyers who indicated the listing was not a good fit toward the bottom. Call, text, and/or email every buyer who showed interest, and offer more information, a second visit, and ask whether that buyer is ready to make an offer. For buyers who indicate no interest in the house, schedule an appointment to meet with them to discuss the buyers' needs and to show the buyers other properties. If the buyer does not answer or respond to your contact attempts, place the buyer into an MLS auto-update for similar homes, and be sure to include a personal message offering to show the buyer any homes in which he or she is interested. Then, add the buyer to your newsletter or a drip campaign so that you'll be top of mind when that buyer is ready to purchase.

If you meet a prospective seller at your open house, follow up right away as well. Offer to make a "house call" including a free, no-obligation analysis of that future seller's home's value. The sooner you are able to personally tour that seller's house, the more likely that seller is to contact you when he or she is ready to sell. Also reach out to every agent with whom an open house visitor told you he or she was working. Often those agents have no idea their buyers have toured your open house, so a call to that agent will spur a communication from the agent to the client, making it that much more likely that buyer will make an offer on your listing.

Make your listing famous

The more exposure you give your listings, the more exposure you are also giving your business. Extensive advertisement of each and every one of your listings beginning with your very first farm-area listing will illustrate to the wider local community that you do more than any other agent to get your listings sold. Advertising extensively requires a larger investment of time and money than many agents are willing to make, but this advertising is essential to maximizing your first listing and every farm-area listing you take thereafter.

In the evolving real estate marketing world, you'll need to stay abreast of all of the newest technologies and you'll need to cast an ever-wider net to garner buyers for your listings. Your advertising efforts should not only include traditional print pieces like postcards, newspaper ads, and brochures, but should also employ the newest marketing tools and technology, such as social media, internet advertising, virtual tours, and videography. Use e-brochures to market your listing to area agents but also pick up the phone to personally invite agents to tour your listings. All of your marketing efforts will help to elevate your image as a farm-area marketing expert, positioning you top of mind for potential future clients.

When those efforts yield results in the form of sold listings, future sellers will begin to take notice. Buyers will also begin to see that since your listings sell quickly, they'll need to contact you to get the inside track on upcoming listings in your farm area. Other agents will begin to recognize you as the go-to agent in your farm area as well, and will begin to contact you when they have buyers looking for a property in your farm area. The harder you work to make your listings famous, the more farm-area recognition you will gain, and the closer you will grow to becoming a famous farmer.

INTERVIEW WITH A FAMOUS FARMER
BILL GASSETT

Bill Gassett is the owner of Maximum Real Estate Exposure and is a real estate veteran. Bill says he has seen it all in real estate, having been through two market crashes and thriving during both. Over the past decade, he has been one of the industry leaders in social media exposure and runs a highly visible website, maxreal-estateexposure.com. His website platform, promising his listings dominant online exposure, has led to his top-producer status in the Metrowest Massachusetts area. Here, Bill shares the keys to his success.

How did you decide to concentrate your business in the Metrowest Massachusetts area?

My farm area is where I grew up, so my name was already somewhat established. I've lived in the area my whole life, so it was a natural fit.

continued

What attracts buyers to your farm area?

It is a highly desirable area with excellent schools, easy access to highways, restaurants, and shopping, as well as other popular attractions such as multiple lakes and a state park.

Tell me a little about how you got your foot in the door as the go-to agent in your farm area.

I started real estate while I was in college and never looked back. I have been promoting myself and my business since I was 19 years old.

Was there any single element you think was most vital to your success?

Most agents, especially when they are new, don't invest enough money into the business. You have to invest to become successful. Every agent should strive to get their name in the spotlight. Name recognition is vital in real estate sales.

What has been your most effective marketing tool?

Without a doubt, mailings have been critical. In addition to sending hundreds of just-listed and just-sold postcards, additional professional postcards are sent quarterly showcasing "why hire Bill Gassett." The internet has also been a way to widen my sphere of influence. My website is one of the most recognized real estate agent sites in the US. I have consistently been writing real estate articles for the past 10-plus years.

My website is now a powerhouse. I also possess strong knowledge of SEO, which helps tremendously with promoting my work.

Harvest your leads

Advertised effectively, every new listing will yield a healthy harvest of buyer and seller leads. You'll meet buyers who are not quite ready to buy but will buy sometime in the future, buyers for whom that particular listing is not quite the right fit, buyers who make an offer on your listing and are outbid but still plan to purchase a home in your farm area, and future seller prospects.

Your lead follow-up can make or break your ability to convert a lead into a future client. Immediately after encountering a lead, record that lead's contact information in a spreadsheet, database, or a contact relationship management system. Include as many details as you can about the lead so that you'll have a good memory of your first interaction the next time you meet or speak with the lead. Set reminders to check in with the lead at least every other month to offer your assistance. Send a monthly real estate market update informing your buyer and seller prospects about changes in market conditions that might affect their timing.

Enter every lead into your newsletter or other drip campaign. If appropriate, follow or friend the lead on social media. The more often you stay in touch with and the more effectively you stay in front of your leads, the more likely those leads are to choose to work with you when they are ready to buy or sell, or to refer to you when they know someone who needs real estate–related assistance.

Develop an agent database

Developing an agent database can be an invaluable marketing strategy for your listing and will help keep you close to the agents most likely to bring you buyers. Keep a running list or database of agents who show your listings, agents whose buyers have come through or sent buyers to your open houses, and those who have sold homes in your farm area. (A good rule of thumb is to add any agent who has sold two or more homes in your farm area within the last two years.) Make note of how the agent likes to be contacted (some have a strong preference for phone, email, or text) and whether the agent has indicated he or she has a buyer looking for a particular home type.

As soon as you sign a new listing agreement and have permission to advertise that listing, give the agents in your database the VIP treatment by sending them early information via e-flyer, social media, personal call, text, or email (or a combination thereof) telling them about your new listing and inviting them to be the first to see or show it—and encourage them to share the information. The agents will appreciate your outreach and will increasingly come to think of you as the go-to agent for your farm area. Your efforts will benefit your sellers as well, as you initiate early marketing buzz for your listing, possibly resulting in a quicker sale.

Don't forget to go to **www.therealestaterainmakers.com** and download a free copy of the *Farming, for Real Estate Agents* workbook to follow along with the exercises.

6

MAKING MARKETING MAGIC

THE MOST SUCCESSFUL agents are also marketing experts. Investing in marketing your listings and your business is essential to achieving continued growth. As you track your budget, you'll likely find that marketing comprises the largest portion of your expenses. However, tracking the actual return on the investment you make in marketing can be difficult, since it's the consistent combination of a variety of marketing efforts over time that yields results. Your marketing plan should include print marketing, online and social media advertising, signage, and personal interaction. There is an old saying in marketing that an effective message needs to be communicated "always, all ways." In real estate, that saying translates into staying in front of potential buyers and sellers anywhere and everywhere they may be. You never know where your next buyer or seller may find you.

Remarketing (repeated advertising delivered via multiple platforms) is an effective method and is widely used by some of the most successful global companies. Take one look at your internet feed and you'll see the same item you searched a week ago pop up on multiple sites you visit online today. Brilliant marketers know that the more often a product appears in front of its intended consumer, the more likely the consumer is to purchase the product.

The same rule applies to your prospective real estate clientele. A prospect may see your sign, then open the mailbox to find your postcard sitting on top of the pile of mail, then open the neighborhood newspaper to see your smiling face on the ad you've placed there, then log on to a favorite social media site to see your latest ad featured in the feed. Is it a sign the prospect should call you? You bet it is. Is the prospect four times more likely to call you than if he or she simply received a single postcard from you? Absolutely.

Print marketing

Print marketing can include postcards, newspaper advertising, advertising in community directories, on community event banners, signage, bus stop ads—anything that requires design, printing, and production falls into this category. Though some print marketing methods may seem antiquated, print marketing remains one of the most effective and proven (albeit the most cost-intensive) components of a successful real estate farmer's marketing cache. Here are some of the print marketing pieces you should include in your plan.

Postcards

Consistent implementation of a direct-mail campaign is key to most dominant real estate farmers' long-term success. If possible, hire a graphic design professional to create your first postcard mailer, which then can serve as a template for future postcards. Your postcards must include your logo and the three essential elements of your marketing message. Next, shop around for the lowest-cost, highest-quality print marketing company you can find. Your time has value and your professional image is essential; money spent on professionally designed and mailed pieces is money well spent. Every marketing piece your farm area sees is a reflection of you, your business model, and how effectively you will market your listings.

Once you have hired a marketing company to design, print, and mail your postcards, that company should automatically remind you monthly when it is time to edit your last card in preparation to send out the next postcard mailing.

A market-update postcard makes a great first mailer. On one side of the postcard, list the twenty most recent farm-area home sales. Include the addresses, the sold prices, the list prices, the types of houses that sold (detached, townhome, condo, etc.), and the number of days the houses were on the market. You can also include additional market statistics such as average sold to list price, average days on market, and average or median sold price for all sold homes on your list. Use the opposite side of the postcard to feature a special offer, a testimonial, or a new listing.

Remember to include your contact information conspicuously on both sides of the postcard along with that all-important call to action. Community residents love to see neighboring homes' sold prices. You'll be amazed to find that farm-area residents begin to collect your market-update postcards to keep track of home sales data.

When you secure your first farm-area listing, your postcard campaign expands. Your ongoing mail campaign should now include a "just-listed" postcard for each new listing, a "just-sold" postcard sent every time you sell a house, and a market-update postcard, special offer, or a proof-of-success piece for months in which you don't have a new listing or sale to advertise (see the following box).

Begin to add photos of your sold homes to the back of your postcard until you have so many that they take the place of your market-update data. Wondering how many pieces to send? A good rule of thumb is to start with 200-300 homes in your farm area and then plan to increase that number by 100 addresses every time you sell a farm-area property. Before long, you'll have the entire farm area covered, and it will be time to think about expanding your farm.

POSTCARD MAILERS

The postcard mail campaign is tried and true and brings results—but like anything else, only when implemented with consistency. Send your postcards at least monthly to achieve the best results. Here are several types of proven direct-mail pieces every farming agent should include in his or her marketing plan.

Just-listed cards: Use these postcards to advertise

each new listing. Each card should include photos of the listing, the address, the price, a brief description of the listing, and a call to action, such as, "Call today to tour this home," or "Contact me today for a free estimate of your home's value." Each piece is meant to target buyers as well as potential future sellers.

Just-sold cards: As soon as your listing settles, market your success. Send a postcard featuring a photo of the sold home, the address, the price for which it sold, and other highlights such as low number of days on the market or high sold-to-list-price ratio. Obtain a brief testimonial from your happy seller to feature on this mailer. Be sure to include another call to action like, "I sold your neighbor's home. I can sell yours, too. Call me today for a free analysis of your home's value!"

Market-update cards: In between just-listed and just-sold cards, send your farm area a card listing the most recent homes sales. Data should include addresses, home type (if your farm includes different types of housing), list price, sold price, and days on market. Remember to include a call to action like, "What is your home worth in today's market? Call me today to find out."

Special-offer postcards: These postcards offer an item of value or a discount and can be co-sponsored by a vendor (a title company, a lender, a contractor) with whom you have a relationship. Perhaps a lender to whom you refer clients wants to offer a free

continued

appraisal or a buyer credit, or your favorite title company wants to offer a $100 settlement fee discount or a free home warranty. You can also consider offering free staging or even a commission dollar discount to your clients for a limited time. Use offers like these to help create a sense of urgency by including a call to action such as, "Limited-time offer. Call today!" You may be required to include an expiration date.

Proof-of-success pieces: Nothing makes a better impression than a testimonial. Has a recent client written a flattering review? Include a photo of the client's house on your postcard with a testimonial so the whole community will see how happy the past client was with your service. Did a recent listing sell for the highest price compared to similar homes in recent history, or faster than other homes, or closer to the asking price than recent sales? If so, use your postcards to highlight those successes, too. Remember to include a call to action: "Want results like these? Call me today."

Promotional items

Some agents supplement their mailers with other direct-mail pieces, including promotional items such as note pads featuring the agent's logo, refrigerator magnets with local sports team or school schedules, pens, kitchen gadgets, or desk calendars. Though these pieces serve as another way to keep your face in front of your community, they can be costly to purchase and to mail. Be sure to choose an item that will have value to your farm-area residents and will end up on the fridge or in the kitchen drawer rather than in the trash.

Newspapers or newsletters

Though wide-distribution papers no longer reach an extensive audience, local papers are often read cover-to-cover, especially when they contain locally engaging stories specific to the area or its residents. Your community newspaper or newsletter can be a great place to market your listings and your business. Advertising in these small, local publications will increase your exposure, and the ad cost is often quite reasonable.

A full-page color ad will make the biggest splash. If a full-page spot isn't available or is not financially feasible, consider a half-page ad on an inside page close to content residents are most likely to read, such as an article covering the most recent community event and featuring photos of community residents. Once you begin to realize revenue from your combined marketing efforts, reinvest by taking out a full-page ad as soon as a spot becomes available, then plan to expand to inside-cover or back-cover placement.

Your newspaper ad should also contain the three elements of your marketing message and must conspicuously display your contact information. Remember to keep your branding consistent, carrying the same logo, look, and basic color scheme through each of your print marketing pieces. Make the most of your newspaper advertising investment by interacting personally with the newspaper's editor. Once you are spending advertising money in a local paper, the editor may be willing to provide you with a little more exposure at no additional charge. Offer to provide the publication's editor with a monthly update of area home sales. Be sure you are given credit for providing the information and can include your contact information in that market update's byline. Remind the editor that you are also happy to provide insights or an interview any time the publication plans to run a real estate–related article.

Signage

Signage is one of the most important components of a real estate farmer's marketing toolbox. All of your signage should include your consistent, recognizable branding and a clearly visible direct phone number. Hang your branded signs prominently in front of your listings, and consider placing a solar-powered light at the base of your sign so it remains visible after dark. During open houses, use branded directional arrow signs at every intersection pointing traffic to your listing. Invest in branded sale arrows to be posted (in compliance with local sign regulations) throughout the farm area, pointing toward each of your listings. You'll know your signage campaign is working when a farm-area resident tells you, "I see your signs everywhere!"

Online marketing

Today's buyers and sellers spend an increasing amount of time online. If you want to be where your potential buyers are, you'll need to spend time online, too. You'll also need to begin to establish a social media presence and a following of your own, which will further reinforce your image as an active farm-area agent. Statistics show that the majority of consumers rely heavily on the internet for selection of any essential service. Whether a potential client is referred to you, personally knows you, or finds you via a print advertisement, you can bet that potential clients will research your services and reviews online. Many of today's buyers and sellers are beginning to search for an agent online without first utilizing traditional methods, so your online presence needs to be powerful.

A vibrant website is essential to your online presence. You don't need to start off with a fancy or expensive website platform, but you do need a website on which potential clients can find you, on which to post information pertinent to your farm, and on which to feature photos of your listings. IDX capability (which enables a website visitor to search the MLS) is ideal. Don't allow yourself to become paralyzed trying to create the perfect site; get a simple site up and running with the key components listed next. Once that site is functioning and once you have the revenue, you will be able to migrate your site to a more complex platform. Be sure to include these components on your site.

Photos

The internet is a visual medium. Consumers visiting real estate sites want to be visually engaged. Nothing is more interesting to real estate consumers than photos of houses. Some website visitors may read paragraphs of text, but they are much more likely to remain engaged if you present them with what they want first: beautiful images of houses you've listed or sold. Better yet, link those photos to additional photos, a video, or a virtual tour to enhance the consumer experience on your site and to keep the consumer on your site longer. Engagement rate is one of the key elements of strong search engine optimization, which will position your site higher in search engine results. Don't have a listing or sale to post yet? Ask another agent at your brokerage if you can feature their listings or recent sales.

Testimonials

Include brief testimonials from past clients, colleagues, or even a friend who can speak to your character. Nothing is more persuasive than kind words praising a positive experience. As you receive additional testimonials, update your site to include those new rave reviews. When a happy client asks how they can thank you, ask them to write a review on your website.

Local information

Illustrate your area expertise by including rich content about what makes your community special. Include a calendar of community events, a history of the community, a community map, and plenty of captioned photos of your farm area. The more locally specific content you include, the more likely you are to be found when a consumer searches using a keyword related to your farm area.

Your marketing message

The three elements of your marketing message—your differentiator, your special offer, and your call to action—should be included on your website. Your website content also needs to constantly be updated. Like engagement rate, consistently updated content improves your website's search engine optimization. Update your special offer at least monthly to help keep content fresh and site visitors excited to return to your site to see what's new.

Your contact information

Many agents make the mistake of creating a phenomenal website and then forgetting the site's purpose. First and foremost, the site should be a way your potential clients can contact you. Your phone number and email address must conspicuously appear on every page of your website. If you are including a contact button, be sure it allows the site visitor to connect with you directly via text, phone, or direct email rather than via a capture form. Though allowing direct contact via a site may permit some spam to come through, wouldn't you rather delete spam than miss a potential lead who wants to speak with you immediately and is turned off by a website form?

Increased traffic is another effective way to improve your site's placement in search engine results. Remember to "point" traffic to your website by always including the URL or a live link to your site on all of your other marketing pieces. When a lead comes in from your website, respond to that lead immediately. Search engines also rank sites based upon site responsiveness to incoming inquiries.

INTERVIEW WITH A FAMOUS FARMER
JEFF KNOX

One of the leading real estate bloggers in the nation, Jeff Knox is a top-producing agent and broker in Dallas, Texas, and author of the book *The Secret to Selling Your Home*. Jeff shares his strategy for using

continued

his website and online presence to dominate a highly competitive farm area.

What made you initially choose to concentrate in your farm area?

The Dallas suburbs have a large footprint. I chose to stay in the area in which I grew up and know best.

What brings buyers to your farm area?

People move to Dallas because there is no state income tax, for industry, and for the weather—and often choose the suburbs for the schools.

How did you get your foot in the door as the go-to agent in your farm area?

For me, it's all SEO (search engine optimization). People believe what they see at the top of the results page, so SEO is the best place to concentrate your efforts. The majority of my leads come from my website.

What do you think was most vital to the success of your website as a lead-generation tool?

It's taken a lot of work—I'm self-taught and started by researching how non–real estate industry consumers searched online to ensure my website would be found using the keywords consumers would use. I stumbled into a group of other agents to bounce ideas off of and used my research and some of those ideas to do all of the SEO work myself. I built my own website and it evolved from there.

What else do you do to maintain your online presence?

Blogging has been 100% the most effective way to increase my presence online. I post three to four articles a week. One of the most important things I'm doing now is video. I have a studio in my office and watch YouTubers to learn about effective delivery and style. I also include video in my drip campaigns. I find that video works among all demographics, since seeing someone's personality before ever meeting the person helps to build trust.

Social media advertising

A solid social media ad campaign will place you in front of your current target market and may bring you additional leads untapped by your other marketing efforts. Like your other campaigns, your social media ads should include the three key elements of your marketing message. Each ad should also contain a lead capture vehicle. Social media is primarily a visual medium, so your ads need to be visually compelling, graphic, and should contain minimal text. The scroll and swipe nature of social media means social media prospects may have shorter attentions spans, so deliver your message as clearly and concisely as possible.

Each ad should include a button or link that leads the prospect to a form that requires an address and email or phone number and will capture lead contact information. Social media platforms often allow the advertiser to control the budget for each ad and offer insights such as views and click-through rate, which can help you refine and develop your ad strategy. Another benefit of this type of advertising is that the ads you place on one platform may automatically feed to other social media platforms. These ads are also designed to remarket your message so that everyone who follows you on your various social media feeds will see your marketing message everywhere they go online, utilizing remarketing to further cement you in their minds as the agent to use when it comes time to buy or sell.

Networking

Networking, otherwise known as word-of-mouth marketing, is one of the most effective and cost-effective ways to get the word out about your listings and your business. The most powerful networkers naturally and almost unconsciously market themselves constantly. If networking doesn't come naturally yet, begin to build the habit by thinking of every social interaction as a networking opportunity.

With this mindset, every trip to the grocery store, to pick the kids up at school, to get your morning coffee, every trip to the gym, every dinner at a restaurant, etc. presents the potential to network. As farm-area residents and professionals within the community begin to recognize you as the local expert, they will inevitably ask you about the market when they see you out and about in the community. When they do, take that opportunity to share information about your new listings and recent farm-area sales and then to ask whether the person who has asked for your insights knows anyone who would benefit from your services.

If you don't already have contact information for the people you meet as you network, ask for their information and add new contacts to your phone or database. Send your contact information to your new connections, too, and watch your business grow.

MARKETING THAT DOESN'T MAKE SENSE

When evaluating the costs of farm-area marketing, take a hard look at the marketing efforts that are most likely to bring you business, and eliminate those that are least likely to bring you a return on your investment. Though many marketing efforts require a financial investment, some costly marketing just doesn't make sense.

Be wary of the many companies that profit from promises of large numbers of leads from their marketing efforts. As you become more visible and successful, you'll inevitably begin to receive calls from salespeople wanting to sell you ad space on everything from shopping carts to city buses to billboards to country club

continued

websites. Taking out an expensive ad on the inside page of a thick community directory that will get lost in a kitchen drawer won't bring much bang for the buck. Investing in a giveaway that is low-quality and will break or might be disposed of is also not a good use of your marketing money.

Before you spend money on any new marketing, do your due diligence and think about those marketing venues from a consumer's perspective—how likely would a buyer or seller be to contact you after seeing your ad in that venue? Is the venue positioning you in front of your targeted customer base or diluting your marketing message? How many other agents are advertising in the same venue? If the answers are unclear, it's best to forego these sales pitches and to invest your money and effort into becoming the best marketer possible to your personal farm area.

Don't forget to go to **www.therealestaterainmakers.com** and download a free copy of the *Farming, for Real Estate Agents* workbook to follow along with the exercises.

7

ESTABLISHING FARM DOMINANCE

BECOMING A DOMINANT farm-area agent means more than just listing and selling homes in the community. True farm-area owners are area experts, serving as resources for and disseminating a variety of information about the farm and its surrounding area as well as market forces affecting the farm area. Dominant agents also develop strong professional relationships, act as matchmakers for their clients, establish strong relationships with other local agents and real estate professionals, and above all become effective rainmakers, generating a consistent stream of leads for themselves and their team members.

Become a consistent resource

As the farm-area expert, you will not only have to be familiar with and informed about news and issues affecting your farm, but you should also be on the front lines of communicating that information and interacting with the organizations that influence or make decisions about farm-area issues. When sharing farm-area news, whether via social media, your website, mailers, or verbally, be sure you are never polarizing or political, that you never "spam" by oversending or oversharing trivial or unimportant information, and that you have fact-checked your information so that you are never seen as an unreliable source.

Consider creating a farm area–centric newsletter to send agents, lenders, and other industry leaders outside of your farm area and in other parts of the country. A brief, photo-heavy e-newsletter with sharable content and links to your website is most effective. This simple monthly communication will pay off in referrals from agents, lenders, and other industry professionals who see you as the go-to agent for your farm area.

Develop professional relationships

Make a concerted effort to develop respectful relationships with agents in your local area. Your competitors may bring buyers to your listings, or conversely may take listings that are a fit for your buyer clients. Always welcome communication from those other agents. Return phone calls promptly and professionally. Thank showing agents for showing your listings and provide prompt and constructive feedback when showing properties listed by other agents.

Keep emotion out of your communications. Build a reputation of integrity composed of ethical behavior, fairness, and honesty. The more respectful and professional your relationships with other agents, the more likely those agents will be to want to work with you. Strong and professional communication with those agents is a benefit to your buyer and seller clients, and to the success of your business.

Be a matchmaker

As you become known as the go-to agent in your farm area, your pipeline will begin to fill with buyer prospects and agents looking for specific property types in your farm area. Keep a running database of these leads, noting the name of the buyer or agent, the buyer's or agent's contact information, and the type of home the buyer or agent is seeking. As soon as you have a new listing, cross-check it against your "buyer and agent looking" database to search for a match. Finding those matches will maximize the price and minimize the days on market for your listings.

As you develop relationships with other local agents, ask to be alerted when those agents have an upcoming listing that might be a match for buyers with whom you are working. When you cannot find a readily available listing that matches the needs of a buyer in search of a farm-area home, it's time to employ your buyer-looking system (see chapter 8). Once you find a match, be sure you advertise your success.

Highlight the advantages of hiring the neighborhood expert

As the expert in your farm, you'll do as much to sell the community as you will to sell individual homes. Farm-area residents will come to recognize that there is a quantifiable advantage to hiring the agent who knows the community better than any other agent—an advantage that puts more eyes on their property and more money in their pockets.

Listing with the agent who possesses nuanced and intimate knowledge of the farm area results in smoother transactions and a better bottom line, since an agent with an investment in the community naturally cares more about property values and can articulate the value of farm-area properties to buyers and their agents. For the buyer, working with the farm-area expert means access to insider knowledge about the community and first access to properties that might be the perfect fit.

Your listing and buyer presentations should highlight the many advantages of hiring the local expert and should include these essential elements, which reinforce the message that you possess the greatest area expertise:

Statistics: Use graphs, charts, and percentages taken from local MLS statistics to visually demonstrate that your listings sell for more money, for closest to asking price, within the shortest timeframe, and/or that you have the most sold farm-area listings. Real data makes a real impact.

Compelling message: Since you have the most listings, you likely also have the most buyers. Promote the advantage of listing with the agent who likely already has a buyer looking for farm-area homes. For buyers, explain the advantages of working with an agent who probably has an upcoming listing that matches the buyer's needs.

Familiar photos: Hire a good photographer to take photos of your farm area at various times of the year, farm-area events, and lots of photos of farm-area properties you've sold. These visual images will help cement your position as the farm-area expert in the eyes of prospective buyers and sellers.

Write in the sky

You've seen those amazing skywriters, the low-flying airplanes that twist and turn, trailing smoke to leave a message scrawled against the bright blue sky. If you've spent time at the beach, you've probably also seen the little planes towing advertising banners across the coastal skyline. Those aerial messages reach an enormous audience simply by being carried at the level of the clouds. In real estate, effective use of social media allows us the same high-level, broad visibility.

Now is the time to increase your social media post frequency across all real estate-appropriate social media platforms. Aim for one post per day, mixing in ample content specific to your farm area. Post about community events, post about a new shop or restaurant that has opened, post an interesting item of local news, post an item about farm-area history, post photos of houses you are preparing to list or have recently sold—if it's about your farm area, post it.

Today's buyers and sellers understand the importance of an agent's strong social media presence, feel connected to agents they see often on social media, and will check to be sure you are active on social media before enlisting your services. They'll be even more inclined to work with you when they see your impressive social media presence.

Make it rain

Real estate is, in truth, the business of lead generation. The most successful real estate rainmakers are lead-generating machines. A strong focus on lead generation is the single most important factor in determining long-term success.

Rainmakers regularly demonstrate their value to the farm area, spend the majority of their time with current and potential clients, and consistently close by asking for the business any time an opportunity presents itself. They also understand that their lead-generation efforts must remain consistent even as they become increasingly busy with clients and transactions.

How will you continue to generate enough leads to ensure a steady flow of transactions? How will you manage new leads as your lead volume increases? The next chapter explores the systems the most prolific real estate rainmakers utilize to ensure long-term success.

Don't forget to go to **www.therealestaterainmakers.com** and download a free copy of the *Farming, for Real Estate Agents* workbook to follow along with the exercises.

8

HARNESSING THE POWER OF FARMING SYSTEMS

NOW THAT YOU have the fundamental elements of a successful real estate farm in place, you'll find your schedule filling with client appointments and settlements. In order to avoid the vacillations in business volume most agents experience as they become busier with revenue-producing activities, you'll need to harness the power of systems that streamline your lead-generation efforts and that efficiently manage leads as those leads come in. Once you have these systems in place, let the systems do the work for you. Many of the systems listed next are simple enough to be delegated to a team member or an assistant and only require consistent repetition to ensure success.

The sphere-of-influence system

Regardless of your years of experience in real estate or your closed volume, you have a core group of friends and family who gleefully sing your praises and will send business your way. You also have a wider circle of acquaintances who are likely to engage your services when they are in need of real estate–related assistance. These groups comprise your sphere of influence.

Maintain a running database consisting of your sphere's names, contact information, and general notes about recent interactions with each member of your sphere. Stay in touch with those closest to you by reminding them how important they are to you and how grateful you are for every referral they send you. Schedule at least monthly calls with the members of your sphere. Schedule time to take members of your sphere to coffee or to lunch, or pop by their homes with a small gift. As you become busier, be sure your sphere remains a priority and that its members know that just because they are seeing your signs everywhere doesn't mean you don't still need their help to build your business. Treat those who helped you get your start better than anyone else and thank them early and often for sending leads your way.

The past-client system

Each time you close a transaction, enter your client's contact information into a database of past clients. Schedule a reminder to follow up with the client four weeks after their sale has closed, then at least every six months. Check in to see how your past client is doing and how they like their new home. Voice-to-voice communication is always most effective. Make the conversation about them, asking for news or updates about their work, their family, or their holidays. Take notes so that next time you check in you'll remember to ask about that new milestone, family member, or trip they have planned. You'll be surprised how often those calls will result in new business for you. Faithful past clients often become your best referrers. They may even tell you they are thinking about purchasing another property or making another move.

Supplement your calls with seasonal gifts. Many agents send a small item like a packet of seeds in the spring and a fun holiday card or ornament in the winter that reinforces the connection and demonstrates to your past client that they are still important to you.

OTHER PEOPLE'S PAST CLIENTS

Here's a seldom-shared insider secret, a method effectively utilized by dominant farm-area agents to grow their client base: when you sell a listing in your farm area, consider entering the buyer of your listing into your past-client system. Statistics show that only 11% of buyers use the same agent for future transactions, so simply by staying in contact with that past buyer (who is now a resident of your farm) you'll position yourself to secure their future listing when they are ready to sell their farm-area home, or to receive referrals from that buyer when they know of other buyers or sellers who would benefit from the services of the farm-area expert.

The referral-rewards system

Every person who refers business your way should be entered into your referral-rewards system. As soon as you are given the referral, send the referrer a handwritten note of thanks along with a small token of your appreciation. Reward the referral, not the result; don't wait for the referred prospect to contact you or for the transaction to settle (although an additional thank you at those times is appropriate too) to thank the referrer. Each contact with the referrer increases the likelihood of that person mentioning you to the prospect or to other potential clients, and thereby increases the possibility of future business.

Your referrers should be considered the VIPs of your database. Be sure to interact with the members of your referral-rewards system personally and often to remind them how grateful you are to them and how important they are to you and your business.

The vendor-referral system

A vendor networking group can be an excellent source of supplements leads. If your farm area already has a community-centric business networking group, join it. If a networking group doesn't already exist in your farm area, create a new group. Start by reaching out to the local business owners in your community and inviting them to join. Make the group interactive, fun, and information-rich so that members come back for more, and be sure the group's focus is building relationships rather than simply swapping referrals. When real relationships are formed, the quantity (and more importantly, the quality) of referrals increases exponentially.

Once established, create a database of networking group members so that you have easy access to member contact information. Consider creating a social media group or page where business group members can post news, special offers, or simply connect. A monthly business group newsletter can be another good way of reminding group members about the specific services each business offers. Some business group members even include reciprocal links to one another's websites or undertake co-marketing efforts.

Always inform a member of your business group when you refer business to them, and remind them to refer back to you. Be sure to thank vendors who have entrusted you with their referrals and to keep them updated on the progress of the referral as the transaction proceeds.

The agent-referral system

A robust agent-referral system can propel your farm-area market share to a new level. To develop an agent-referral network, start by establishing relationships with dominant agents in other real estate markets. The agents most likely to refer to you are those who service the most clients, so go after the big fish. Doing the research is simple and can be delegated to an assistant.

Using the internet, search for real estate agents in major markets, slowly working your way across the country. Use keywords buyers would use to find a real estate agent, then reach out to the agents who have the best online presence. Send each of those agents an email explaining that you are looking for an agent to whom to refer buyers interested in purchasing in their market areas, and let them know you will follow up with a phone call. If the agent doesn't respond, that may be an indicator the agent won't be responsive to a referral you send, so you may want to move on to the next agent in that market.

When you connect with a responsive agent, ask the agent whether he or she already has a referral relationship with an agent in your farm area. If not, ask the agent whether he or she would be interested in an exclusive reciprocal referral arrangement with you. Under the terms of this arrangement, you would send every referral for that agent's market area to that agent and that agent would in turn send any referral in your market area to you exclusively.

Keep a database of the agents who agree to be part of your referral system, and create a simple e-newsletter to send each member of this database quarterly. The newsletter should serve as a reminder that you are the expert in your farm area and should contain a brief local market update, a few seasonal photos of your farm area, and a link to an article your agent network might find interesting or might want to share with their audience. Be sure to follow the members of your agent referral system on social media and remind them to follow you back. Treat the agents in your referral network as you would any referrer; when an agent-referral system member refers business to you, thank them promptly and keep them updated as the transaction progresses.

The expireds system

When executed well and consistently, the expireds system can be one of the most profitable and productive systems in your arsenal. Expired listings are the "low-hanging fruit" of the real estate farm. Sellers whose listings have expired not only have already indicated their desire to sell, but they are also likely frustrated by their failed listing. These sellers are in genuine need of a capable agent who will succeed in selling their house. The first agent in the door of an expired listing often secures that future listing.

Implementation of the expired system starts with research. Begin by searching the MLS for recently expired listings. Now, set your MLS to update you as future listings in your farm area expire. Create a database of these listings including the property address, seller names, and seller contact information. Next, get in front of those expired sellers as early as you can.

First, drop by the house with an eye-catching marketing piece, your listing presentation, or a giveaway, and have your elevator pitch ready. When the seller answers the door, introduce yourself and ask the seller whether he or she still intends to sell. Regardless of the answer, ask a few questions about what their listing experience was like: How many showings did they have? What type of feedback did they receive? Did they get any offers while they were listed?

Never denigrate the last listing agent; instead, listen and then give the seller a compelling reason to consider listing with you. Do you have the best percentage of listings to sales? Highlight that. Have you sold more expired or withdrawn homes than any other agent in your market area? That's compelling. If you lack motivating statistics, extend a limited-time special offer, then ask for an appointment to sit down with the seller to review your full marketing strategy.

If the seller isn't ready to relist, stay in front of that seller with a series of direct-mail pieces that reinforce your compelling message and contain a clear call to action. Be consistent and persistent with your expired system mailings. Statistics show that only 50% of agents mail to sellers with expired listings more than twice. Only 25% mail more than three times. However, on average, eight repetitions of a marketing piece are necessary to firmly grab a prospect's attention. If you are the first agent in the door and the agent mailing to the expired prospect eight or more times, you are likely the last agent standing—and you have the very best odds of obtaining the listing when the seller is ready to relist.

The FSBO system

Like the expired system, the "for sale by owner" (FSBO) system is a great way to engage prospects who have already indicated their desire to sell. Unlike the expired system, FSBOs often have unrealistic expectations about what is required to successfully sell a house.

Obtaining FSBO business begins by establishing a relationship with the seller while demonstrating value and at the same time allowing the seller to experience the challenges of attempting to sell without an agent. Most FSBOs do not understand that the price at which their house is listed must reflect the fact that there is no commission being paid to a listing agent, and that savvy buyers will therefore expect a discount. FSBOs may also be slow to realize that many buyers' agents shy away from showing for-sale-by-owner properties, since the lack of a listing agent results in the buyers' agent doing the work of two agents. Together with the relatively limited market exposure a

FSBO is able to achieve, the enormous liability inherent in selling a home by owner, and the time and effort a successful home sale requires, the vast majority of FSBOs eventually realize the value of enlisting a real estate agent.

The agent who engages the FSBO early and often has the best chance of obtaining the listing when the FSBO finally becomes exhausted and frustrated. Be sure you are driving or walking the streets of your farm area frequently so that you'll always know when a new FSBO puts that little "sale" sign up in the yard. As you find FSBOs in your farm area, enter the FSBO's address and contact information (easy to find in the FSBO's ad or on the small yard sign) into your FSBO system database. Begin with a visit to the house to preview it for potential buyers for whom the house might be a good fit and to explain the FSBO Fair Trade (see the following box), then follow up with phone calls every week offering your assistance until the FSBO engages you to list and sell.

THE FSBO FAIR TRADE

New FSBOs are often hesitant to even speak with a real estate agent. They've decided to try to sell on their own for a reason. Perhaps the FSBO believes he or she will save money, time, or the perceived hassle of dealing with a "pushy salesperson." Whatever the reason, the FSBO undervalues the expertise of a real estate professional. Approaching the seller as a resource and

continued

a partner by introducing the FSBO Fair Trade can help to correct FSBO misperceptions and help to build a trusting relationship. Here's how it works:

The FSBO Fair Trade offers the seller many of the benefits of working with a listing agent but at no cost or obligation to the seller. You'll agree to provide the seller professional consultation services including advice about how to best present and show the house, advice about how to effectively market the house, updates on real estate market conditions, advice about how to evaluate offers, and advice about how to calculate the proceeds from the sale. You'll agree to provide referrals to other real estate–related professionals the seller might need to engage, and you'll provide answers to questions the seller might have throughout the course of the transaction. In exchange, you'll leave a guest registry at the house or a QR code through which buyers can register electronically so that you may follow up with potential buyers. The guest registry is also an added security measure, since it will collect contact information for everyone who tours the house.

Each week, arrange to stop by to pick up the guest registry or call to touch base and to chat with the seller, answering any seller questions. During these visits or conversations, you'll further cement your relationship with the seller, you'll gain new buyer leads, you may potentially find a buyer for the FSBO—and you'll be positioned to list the house when the seller is ready.

The buyer-looking system

As soon as you encounter a buyer looking for a property in your farm area, begin a letter campaign searching for properties not yet on the market that match the buyer's needs. The letter should be brief, compelling, and as specific as possible. Set a goal to send fifty letters each week, working your way through all of the farm-area properties that match your buyer's needs until you've mailed to each one.

Not only are you going the extra mile turning over rocks to find the buyer a house, but you may even secure a listing if the house doesn't work for your buyer or if your buyer has already found another house by the time the potential seller contacts you. Have a buyer looking in an area outside of your farm? Send letters to that neighborhood as well. Once you sell a few houses in other areas, you may be on your way to expanding to your next farm.

Rental systems

The rental system is composed of two components: an absentee-owner system and a tenant system. We'll review the absentee-owner system first.

The absentee-owner system

This system targets the owners of non-owner-occupied properties. To implement this system, scour your MLS to find homes that have absentee owners. Create a database of these homes listing the property addresses, owner names, and owner addresses. Mail to this group monthly using a simple postcard campaign.

Since these owners may have never lived in your farm area or might have been absentees for a lengthy period, it's important that your mailings prove your local market expertise.

Your market knowledge and track record might not be as obvious to this group as it would be to your farm-area residents, so be sure to list recent farm-area sales data as well as photos of homes in your farm area you have recently sold. Highlighting low inventory, low number of days on market, or sales for above asking price can be persuasive evidence to an absentee owner that it might be time to cash in on an investment property. Your call to action to this group should include a free CMA, since absentee owners are often curious about the current value of their investment property and often have no first-hand knowledge of farm-area sales. If you are the agent who sends an absentee owner good news about value or current local market conditions, you are that much more likely to secure the listing when that owner is ready to sell.

The tenant system

Now that you have created a list of non-owner-occupied houses, you are positioned to mail to the tenants residing in those properties. Include any rental apartments in your farm area as well. The goal of the tenant system is to demonstrate the value of home ownership. Each month, mail a direct-marketing piece to your tenant list (you can use "Neighbor At" in lieu of a name in the address field since tenant names can be difficult to obtain). Mailing pieces might highlight low mortgage interest rates, the true cost of renting, the differential between rental money spent and equity built in an owned home, or rates of home-value appreciation. The resonant message should be the value of owned real estate as a sound investment as well as a home.

Your favorite mortgage lender can provide data to include in these mailings. A lender can also be a good partner with whom to "tag team" to land prospects currently renting and considering a purchase. The agent in front of a tenant when he or she is ready to put down roots in your farm area is the agent most likely to secure that tenant as a future buyer. If you find a tenant is not quite ready to buy, needs to save for a down payment, needs to pay off debt, or needs to improve credit, work with a lender or financial planner to assist that tenant toward reaching the goal of home ownership and you'll have a client for life.

PAYING FOR LEADS

We know it's tempting—pay a fee to an online service for leads that are "guaranteed" to pay off in triple the investment. Too good to be true? Of course it is. The quality of these leads is often so poor that even with the promptest and most effective follow-up they rarely result in actual business. Reliance on these services for leads may also prevent you from learning the single most important skill a real estate agent can possess and the skill that most directly correlates with long-term success (you guessed it): lead generation.

continued

Not only will paying for leads be an exercise in frustration, it will quickly drain your marketing budget and will hamstring your ability to invest in marketing your own business. The bottom line is: if you have what it takes to be successful in real estate, you should never need to pay for leads.

Don't forget to go to **www.therealestaterainmakers.com** and download a free copy of the *Farming, for Real Estate Agents* workbook to follow along with the exercises.

9

EXPANDING YOUR FARM

NOW THAT YOU have established dominance in your farm area, it may be time to think about expanding your farm. Through these pages, you've developed a duplicatable recipe for success, which can now be applied to almost any other area. Begin to look for nearby, similar fields in which to begin to sow new seeds. Is there a geographic area adjoining your primary farm that might be a good choice? Perhaps a similar-style community makes sense to target? Does a nearby city, suburb, or community feel like a good fit? As you did with your primary farm, analyze historical sales data, vet the competition (revisit chapter 1 for a refresher), and get to know as much as you can about that new potential farm prior to committing effort and funds to expansion.

Though some real estate farmers feel capable of taking on a new farm area themselves with use of the systems outlined previously and the support of a solid administrative staff, others find that bringing on a team member who is a resident of the new area makes the most sense. Adding a team member to help you farm the new area can help offset some of the financial and time obligations that accompany expansion. Whichever path you choose, as with any business expansion, you'll need capital, time, and effort in order to grow. This chapter explores the key elements of a successful expansion.

Investors

As you expand your farm, your marketing efforts must also expand. Additional print ads, more direct mail and postcards, additional signage, more social media advertising, and increased sponsorships and events within the new farm area will be necessary. Increased marketing means increased expenses. The best way to offset some of these expenses and at the same time to build relationships with other real estate industry professionals is to find investors.

Who should your investors be? Anyone who might benefit from your referrals or the exposure your marketing can provide is a good candidate. Lenders you trust, local title companies, insurance or home warranty companies, financial planners, stagers and decorators, home improvement contractors, and anyone else with whom you have a trusting professional relationship and whom you are comfortable endorsing via shared advertising might be a good fit.

These professionals should be considered more than just co-advertisers; since your success is vital to their success, consider them investors in your business. The more leads generated by your joint efforts, the more both of your businesses grow. Always remember to work with your broker and your investors' compliance departments to be sure you are RESPA compliant and in compliance with local and federal laws and agent organizations rules.

Seminars

When breaking into a new farm area, it is vital to get in front of your new farm-area residents as quickly as possible. Consider a seminar with an interesting and relevant real estate–related topic such as how to prepare a house for sale, how to get pre-approved for a loan, or how to make a house-to-house move. Bring a lender along to help residents evaluate whether they need to sell their current homes in order to buy a new home.

Are there rental units within your farm area? If so, consider a seminar discussing the benefits of purchasing versus renting. Is the farm area composed mainly of "forever" homes? Perhaps a seminar about updating or preparing to downsize in which you offer a free consultation to potential future sellers is a good idea. Do residents of your community show interest in buying second homes, flips, or rental properties? If so, host a seminar about real estate investing, and invite a title company and tax accountant to answer legal and tax-related questions. Whichever subject you choose, with a little free food or beverages and meaty content, a seminar is a good way to get to know the residents in your new farm area who might be most imminently interested in buying or selling.

Economical advertising

Your print ads, postcard campaigns, social media efforts, signage, and sponsorship of community events all reinforce your image and have a long-term cumulative effect. When committing to advertise in a new farm area, be as good a negotiator for yourself as you are for your clients. Contract for your newspaper ads for at least a full year to get the very lowest rate possible. Offer to sponsor multiple community events and negotiate a bundled sponsorship fee for those events. Shop for the highest-quality, lowest-cost company to produce your postcard mailers. Be wise about spending your advertising dollars while keeping your long-term vision in mind—and remember that repetitive marketing over time yields the best results.

Make communication your priority

As your farm expands, you'll need to become a masterful communicator. Quick response time is key. A timely answer to a call, text, or email can mean the difference between a potential buyer or seller working with you or moving on to another agent, an agent encouraging his or her buyer to make an offer on your listing or that of another agent, or a small issue becoming a major problem.

A very successful real estate farmer who dominated her real estate farm in the days before texting existed once told the story of a time she was so busy that she had no choice but to let her voicemail fill up and leave her emails unanswered. She felt so overwhelmed that instead of filtering through the backlog of voicemails and emails or delegating that task, she simply deleted them all. Imagine the potential business she lost through that simple act.

Whenever possible, pick up your phone. Voice-to-voice contact remains the most efficient and effective means of communication. If you cannot answer a call, text the caller that you will call him or her back as soon as you are able. Whenever possible, respond to a lead, client, or another agent by the same means with which they have initiated contact. Reply to any call, text, or email no more than an hour or two after that communication is received. Especially in a new farm area, one missed call can mean a missed opportunity to secure a listing that may lead to multiple future buyer and seller leads. Keep your phone by your side, your voicemail cleared, and your focus on communication.

Take advantage of opportunities

The most fruitful farmers are always on the lookout for potential opportunities. Plan any expansion with your eyes wide open. Keep track of local agents who may be phasing out of farm areas in which you want to expand. Think about whether it might make more sense to build a relationship with that agent and to possibly offer a structured buyout or simply to move in to the new area as the agent moves out. Is a change like a relocation of a major employer on the horizon for a nearby or similar farm area? If so, residents might see the advantage of selling while their market is hot, and there may be room for you to gain market share as inventory increases. You might also consider approaching a large local employer to offer to become part of a relocation network or service to incoming employees.

Create a list of areas into which it might make sense to expand, create a list of questions you need to answer prior to committing to expansion, and then create an action plan for steps you need to take to gain market share in your new farm area. Whether simply replicating the steps you used to dominate your current farm, finding investors, adding seminars or new sponsorships and activities within the new farm, or reaching out to agents who might be phasing out of the farm, always track your progress and monitor the effectiveness of your efforts.

Don't forget to go to **www.therealestaterainmakers.com** and download a free copy of the *Farming, for Real Estate Agents* workbook to follow along with the exercises.

10

TEAM FARMING

ANY GOOD FARMER knows that when the seeds have been planted and the soil is fertile, the time will soon come to harvest the crops. That means it's also time to harness even more horsepower; it's time to enlist help. Effective delegation, partnerships with the right people, and continued evolution as your business grows are essential to continued success.

Learn to delegate

Think of delegation as the best investment you can make in your time budget, and the one that will yield the greatest return. Now is the time to revisit your time-blocking and to carefully analyze each activity. Place an asterisk next to any activities highlighted in blue that do not necessarily require your expertise, time, or personal execution. Can someone else be trained to create your postcards, to draft your marketing brochures, to post to your social media accounts, or to coordinate contractor appointments? Chances are the answer is yes.

With a little investment of time spent training an assistant or apprentice, you'll find your efficiency and productivity increase exponentially as your available time for revenue-producing activities increases. You'll also find you are free to devote more of your valuable time to those activities highlighted in yellow and purple, the activities that will yield the greatest balance and personal rewards.

Hire an assistant

Identify an assistant you can entrust with all of the "behind the scenes" processes that keep your business running. Since you'll need time to train your new assistant, be sure to start this process at a relatively quiet time of the year. Your assistant should be trained to complete any office-related tasks such as ordering supplies and maintaining technology, sending mailings, overseeing print campaigns, managing your website and social media, and running the portions of your lead-generation systems that do not require your personal attention. This will free you to interface with your clients. Client interface is the one task that should never be delegated to an assistant (remember, your client hired you).

As you train your assistant, ask that they carefully document each step in each process and create a daily schedule. This will enable you to efficiently pass the information along to a new assistant or an additional assistant should you need to do so. Choose your assistant with care; they should be as detail- and quality-oriented as you are and should consider themselves a partner in your business, since everything your assistant does reflects upon you and affects your reputation.

Recruit or train buyers' agents

When your systems are working and your farm begins to generate more leads than you can handle, it's time to consider bringing on buyers' agents to handle your overflow leads. Instead of letting internet leads, sign calls, and buyer inquiries pile up while you are in client appointments, position your buyers' agents to receive new leads so that they can follow up right away. The quicker the response, the more likely you are to secure the business.

Your buyers' agents can also help conduct open houses during times when you have multiple opens scheduled at the same time. When you do have multiple opens with team members covering each open house, it's a good idea to "float" between properties so that you'll have a personal interaction at each, allowing you personal insight into buyer traffic and response as well as first-hand follow-up with your seller after each open concludes.

Consider a listing partner

As your farming systems generate a multitude of listing leads, you may also need to enlist help to sustain the excellent level of service your seller clientele has come to expect. Ideally, your listing partner should share your work ethic, put forth the same image of professional expertise you do, and inspire the same level of trust in your clientele. Choose this person carefully, and be sure to work side by side with your new listing partner until you are confident that they will afford the same level of service your clients have come to expect from you.

Your listing partner should also ideally possess a skill set that is complementary to your own. Maybe you are an excellent marketer and your listing partner is a fabulous negotiator. Perhaps your listing partner has insight into the latest trends in social media while you are better at personal follow-up. Whatever the dynamic, employing the right listing partner should empower you to work more efficiently and effectively as well as to take on more business as you divide and conquer, thereby increasing your ability to expand your business.

Hire specialists

Once you have the key team members in place to run the administrative aspects of your business, to take on overflow buyer leads, and to assist you with listings, you'll need to delegate the more specialized areas of your services wisely. The following roles are key.

Marketing designer

This person should be capable of taking your vision for print marketing and turning it into a reality. Your marketing designer should be able to produce and deliver mailers (including letters and postcards); to produce newspaper, magazine, and other ads; to design promotional pieces and logos; and to be sure your branding is consistently implemented throughout all marketing campaigns. Ideally this person will be familiar enough with your systems and the print media necessary for each system to be able to remind you when it's time to create, edit, approve, or to send a new piece.

Social media expert

This person should help you keep your social media accounts up to date, provide ideas for new posts, share ways to interact with other influencers, and even post on your behalf as appropriate. Your social media expert should be adept at the use of all appropriate social media platforms and aware of changes and developments in social media that could influence your business.

Organizer

An organizer can be an integral member of a high-functioning, full-service real estate team. The organizer meets with a client to assist in reducing clutter, deciding what to take to a new home, and prepares the house for the staging process. A good organizer can help a seller feel much less overwhelmed while vastly reducing premarket preparation time. This person can also offer services to buyers as they prepare to move into a new home.

Stager

This person should have an excellent eye for interior design and should understand buyers' perceptions of properties. Ideally, they should have an inventory of furniture and accessories ready for use to stage a new listing. They should also be skilled at communicating effective presentations to property owners, be able to convey the value of a well-staged house for the duration of the marketing period, and be able to persuade the seller to make any necessary changes to the property to position it so that it presents with maximum appeal and attains maximum value.

Photographer

Listing photos create a make-or-break first impression and often dictate how many buyers tour your listings. These photos also reflect the quality of your marketing and therefore your image as a professional, so be sure your photographer is top-notch. Often, buyers refuse to even look at a house that could be a good fit for them because the photos viewed online are so unappealing. Choose an excellent professional photography company, ideally one that also offers virtual tours, floor plan imaging, aerial photography, and videography options. Listing photography is one area in which you should plan to invest a little more in order to obtain the very best possible outcome for your sellers, which will in turn result in additional repeat and referral business for you.

Coach

Many of the most successful agents continue to evolve by working with a real estate coach. An ideal coach is a seasoned real estate veteran who serves as a cheerleader, mentor, sounding board, accountability partner, and an inspiration. The coach you choose should have a proven track record, a sound following, and should be accessible. Though the investment in a coach can be sizeable, many agents attest that working with a real estate coach is the key to taking their businesses to the next level.

INTERVIEW WITH A FAMOUS FARMER
KENDYL YOUNG

Kendyl Young is a top-producing team leader in Glendale, California. Every agent on her team is coached to hone negotiating, marketing, and business skills to their clients' advantage. Here, Kendyl shares how she selected her farm, built her business, and how coaching has helped her stay at the top of her market.

How did you select your farm area?

My farm was the neighborhood I dreamed of living in from an early age. Mother was a real estate agent and I would visit her at the office. The area around her office was like a dream to me—green, gently sloping tree-lined avenues filled with adorable homes all perfectly maintained and with lots of character. To an urban kid from a working-class neighborhood, it was the definition of "arrived." I bought a home right on that street and started farming there from my first day in Glendale.

What is special about your farm area?

Northwest Glendale is uncommonly beautiful. The streets are lined with mature shade trees and many of them flower, especially the jacarandas. The homes were built in the 1930s and are variations of character

continued

homes—identifiable architectural styles like Spanish, English, ranch, and more. They blend together in an area with soul, personality, and charm. Brand Park and the Brand Library are city treasures, and Kenneth Village provides a central gathering place that brings the community and neighbors together.

How did you secure your first buyer or seller client in your farm area?

I started holding any open house and working with any client I could get. I had a new baby at home, but I still grabbed an open house nearly every weekend. I was dead sure I would meet a "real" buyer every single time . . . and most times I did. As I progressed, I worked up the courage to door-knock. I worked up to a routine of knocking five days a week, three hours a day. I kept track of any conversation and opportunity that I discovered and worked hard to follow up and be valuable to whomever I met. I am a terrible salesperson, but a great relationship builder.

Eventually I bought a billboard (horrifying but effective) and launched a direct-mail campaign. The billboard is mentioned to this day, though it was removed long ago. Building relationships, being the absolute expert in the area, and treating everyone with respect was vital to my early success.

Did a mentor or coach help you in any way?

Yes. I always went to the "seminars" where the guru

du jour would do a big rah-rah training, and then sell the books and tapes in the back. In the early '90s I had my first coach—it was group coaching, and it was career-changing for me. Turns out I love structure, routine, and accountability. I also love learning. I got my first one-on-one coach in the early 2000s, and I've coached continually since then.

Is there anything else you would like to share?
I doubt I would have expanded my farm if I had stayed a single agent. The added expansion that comes with the visibility of a brokerage has been very helpful. I use retargeting digital ad products to keep my name in front of my farm and I am very active on social media. I also focus on my clients' hopes, dreams, and aspirations. What are they afraid of and what value can you bring that is about THEM, not you?

As your business grows, you may also need to employ additional assistants to help with paperwork and post-contract details. Constantly monitor your own activities for tasks that could be better delegated to someone else so that your time is spent on revenue-producing activities and servicing your clients' needs.

Don't forget to go to **www.therealestaterainmakers.com** and download a free copy of the *Farming, for Real Estate Agents* workbook to follow along with the exercises.

11

BECOMING A FAMOUS FARMER

WHAT FEELS BETTER than walking down the street, into your favorite restaurant, or even into the grocery store, and having people know immediately who you are? You'll know you've reached a certain level of recognition when people you don't know tell you they recognize you from somewhere, or that they see your signs everywhere, or even greet you by name. I remember the first time I was at our neighborhood coffee shop and a mom whispered to her little boy, "You know who that is, right?" I had no idea she was referring to me until the little boy came up to me and asked, "Can I have your autograph, Meredith Fogle?"

Admittedly, being the locally famous king or queen of your farm area doesn't exactly make you a Kardashian, but it certainly keeps you top of mind for people who want to buy and sell. Having a name that resonates within your local business and real estate community can be immensely helpful to your business and reputation as a whole. So, how do you become a famous farmer? If you've followed the steps in this book so far, you're well on your way. The next step is to become your own best publicist. Follow this strategy and you'll find notoriety in no time.

Be as visible as possible

Real estate remains one of the only industries in which its professionals' marketing includes their own images, so make sure that image is one you want everyone to see. Hire an excellent photographer to take your photo, and place that photo in front of your target audience through every available avenue.

Until you have the income to support hiring someone to help you with publicity, you'll need to act as your own publicist. Be sure your yard signs have your image emblazoned upon them. Send branded mailers every month. Include your photo in all of your advertisements. Purchase banners (yes, with your photo on them) to hang at the community events you sponsor. Consider advertising on community bus stops, grocery carts, or movie screens. Offer to appear as a guest contributor on a local television show. When you do, be sure to share the clip of your appearance everywhere you can (on social media, on your website, on your company's website, etc.).

Video can be a great way to get your brand and your image out there, too. Consider hiring a professional videographer to create a profile piece for you to send to prospects and to promote on social media. The more your image is "out there" in your farm area, the more locally famous you will become.

Get people talking

There's no better way to build your reputation than to get other people talking about you. Begin by asking for testimonials. Every time you transact with a client, ask that client to provide a review of your service. To make it easy for the client to provide a review, send him or her a link to the site on which you hope the client will post the review along with a reminder that five stars plus a written review will give your business the biggest boost.

Make it easy for the client to refer you as well. Tell the client how thrilled you would be to provide the same exceptional service you provided the client to a client's friend or family member. Remind the client that a referral is the highest compliment you can receive. Add a sentence to the end of every email asking your contacts to keep sending referrals your way.

Show up and get personal

Do you ever notice that celebrities promote their latest projects by visiting the biggest network talk shows and morning shows? Why? It's in their contract—because the studios know that putting their headliners in front of the largest possible audiences in a semi-casual setting will make audience members feel that they know the celebrity on a more intimate level. That feeling of personal connection makes audience members that much more likely to buy tickets to the celebrity's latest film.

Successful farmers know that they, too, need to put themselves in front of as a large an audience as possible and that they must build personal connections. If you are not naturally outgoing and sociable, you'll need to learn to embrace social opportunities. Join or create farm-area clubs or a neighborhood business group; attend neighborhood meetings and events; accept invitations to every party you receive; and attend holiday gatherings, business openings, performances, and sporting events. Opportunity is most likely to happen when you find yourself in the right place at the right time with the right people—so it stands to reason that you'll give yourself the greatest possible opportunity by being around as many people in as many places as practical as often as possible.

Host community events

One fun and effective way to get in front of farm-area residents is to host a community event. Find out what your community is already doing and events for which a host or sponsor might be needed. Find out which events your community isn't conducting yet but would like to plan. Look into activities hosted by similar communities and suggest those to your community planners, or take the bull by the horns and initiate a new event yourself. Market the event as widely as possible to ensure the greatest attendance. Marketing efforts should include use of social media, mailers or personal invitations, neighborhood signs, banners, message boards, and the community grapevine.

When hosted in concert with your HOA or another community organization, that organization might help to subsidize the cost of the event and will certainly help to publicize it. Whether you are hosting a 4th of July cookout, a chili cook-off, a Super Bowl party, a Memorial Day bash, a wine tasting, a casino night, a movie night, or another unique event, the goal should be to provide a fun activity, to attract a large and diverse crowd, and to give you the opportunity to meet new residents and become better acquainted with the residents you've already met.

Get to know other key community members

Once you become known as the "king" or "queen" of your farm area, it's important to connect with other key figures and decision makers in the community. Take the time to have an in-person conversation over coffee or lunch with the local mayor, the president of the HOA or condo board, the person who runs your community management company, and any other locally recognized key business people or community leaders. Developing relationships with these community members will help ensure you are kept abreast of issues and changes affecting your farm area that may also affect the real estate market and property values. It will also increase the likelihood that you will be asked to get involved when and as needed, and that these key (and very connected) community members will think of you when they hear about someone wanting to buy or sell in your community.

Blog

Keep your farm area interested and engaged by blogging about locally important issues and events. Share stories about your farm area, farm-area news, industry news that might be interesting or important to community residents, and topics and ideas discussed at your seminars as blog content. Engage your audience by inviting interaction with and questions from community residents. Use a "something new every day" approach, keeping your blog fresh and interesting. Ask the community leaders you've come to know to keep you informed of upcoming news and events so you can share the information in your blog.

Become a social media star

If posting daily to the major social media outlets isn't your forte, hire someone who is great at it. Avoid companies who produce cookie-cutter posts. Instead, post content that shows your personality. Include "lifestyle" images that capture you doing what you do best behind the scenes. Unless you are a selfie-master, ask someone else to photograph you holding an open house, showing a house to a buyer, presenting a contract, prepping a listing, on the phone at your office—people love to see you in action. Be careful not to be too selfie-heavy, however. Your followers want to see glamour shots of your listings, not just of you. Follow the "rule of thirds" when posting to social media: one-third of your posts should be promotional (advertising your listings, your sales, or another success), one-third should offer a resource (a real estate market or mortgage trend update, a link to a useful real estate–related article, or a helpful tip or piece of advice), and one-third should be personal (a lifestyle image or video). Most social media platforms allow you to share your content to other platforms, saving you time and effort.

Finally, follow your friends, past clients, local organizations, local agents, and other real estate industry influencers. Those you follow will likely follow you back, further enhancing your social media presence. Follow these steps and you'll have a recipe for becoming a social media "influencer"—and someone people in your farm area and beyond will follow and will recognize.

INTERVIEW WITH A FAMOUS FARMER
ANITA CLARK

A top-producing Georgia real estate agent and prolific blogger, Anita Clark has used social media and blogging to build and expand her business. Her blog, https://sellingwarnerrobins.com, includes local real estate market updates, local history, descriptions of and updates about the subdivisions she farms, and a calendar of local activities and events. Here, Anita lets us in on the secrets of her success.

How did you discover blogging as a marketing tool?

I became an agent during the market crash in 2007 and I was looking for a way to stand out among my peers. Pretty much by accident I stumbled upon marketing via the web and how to focus on providing subdivision information that area consumers were actively seeking. Online blogging led to social media marketing as well as print media. Those helped establish my brand and have driven a lot of business my way over the past decade.

continued

Was there any single element you would identify as most vital to your success?

Establishing my own Wordpress blog that I controlled was the catalyst that pushed sales up and generated a lot of new prospects. I would say blogging about both local and national real estate–related content has been most vital. Many of my clients say they find me online then choose me because of reviews.

Your website lists several area subdivisions in which you specialize. Have you expanded your farm area over time?

I live in my farm area and I have since branched out to other "farms" within my county. Robins Air Force Base is within 15 miles of nearly everywhere I market to. With over 20,000 employees, it is a fertile farm. Figuring out what types of print media were effective in my area, blogging to consumer needs, and using social media to get my brand to a wider audience have had the most impact.

What do you do to stay involved in or to give back to your farm area?

I help out through my church. It is a wonderful outlet with plenty of opportunities to assist others.

Were you given any advice that helped you along the way?

A very successful agent in town pulled me aside early on and told me to find my niche and make it my own. I have always remembered that advice.

Looking back, is there anything you would do differently?

Probably not. I am happy with the course of my career and having had such a tremendous opportunity to assist so many local buyers and sellers.

Be professionally impeccable

Once you've achieved status as the dominant agent in your farm, your reputation becomes infinitely more important. The saying, "The higher you fly, the bigger the target on your back," is true. The more visible you are, the more your colleagues and your community will be watching to be sure you are maintaining your professional integrity, so be professionally impeccable. What does professional impeccability mean? First and foremost, conduct your business ethically. Be honest. Put your clients' needs ahead of your own. Never criticize your competitors. Live by the golden rule. Keep your focus on building your business, fulfilling your clients' goals, and giving back—and the rest will fall into place.

Give back

When run properly, genuinely, and generously, your farm will yield immeasurable rewards, both professionally and personally. Giving back to the farm area that gives you so much is both important and rewarding. Giving back to your farm can take on many iterations. For some farmers, giving back means serving on a community organization like an HOA or neighborhood school PTA. For others, giving back means working with a charitable organization or chairing a charitable event that brings the community together to benefit a cause or another population.

Not sure what to do to give back? Contact your community managers or leaders to ask whether there is a need or put a message out on social media to find out how you can help. Volunteering in your farm can work wonders. If a large volunteer contingent does not already exist, consider creating one; not only will your community benefit, but you will be recognized as the founder of a meaningful cause. Start small, but start somewhere. Giving back to your community is one of the most important aspects of being a successful and productive real estate farmer.

Don't forget to go to **www.therealestaterainmakers.com** and download a free copy of the *Farming, for Real Estate Agents* workbook to follow along with the exercises.

12

SELLING YOUR FARM

A SUCCESSFUL REAL estate farm is a valuable and trad-
able commodity. The database you've built, the relationships
you've formed, the track record you've established, and the
reputation you have achieved are valuable assets. The future
income potential of your farm area also has value. There will
come a time when you are ready to step back from the rainmaker role and to reap the rewards of your years of hard work.
When that time comes, don't allow your farm to fall fallow and
die. Find another fabulous farmer or farmers who can keep
your farms running—and keep proceeds from your farm flow-
ing to you even as you phase out of farming.

Real estate farms are traditionally sold using one of two
methods. In either scenario, you'll need to be prepared to quantify the value of your business and its income potential. It's a
good idea to work with a financial planner, tax accountant,
and/or an attorney to be sure the valuation is accurate and that
the sale is completed in a financially and legally sound manner.

The fixed-price one-time sale

Here, the real estate farmer cleanly hands off the business to the farmer who will step into the business. The databases, marketing methods and pieces, and all related systems are transferred to the new farmer via a fixed-price one-time sale. In this method, it's essential that the infrastructure be completely in place to ensure a smooth transition. Elements of the transition plan should include whether the new farmer will take over your existing physical office location; whether existing team members and administrative staff will transition to the new farmer; whether the new farmer will continue to utilize your website, social media, photography, staging, and other internal resources and outside specialists; and how the hand-off will be communicated to your past clients, prospects, and sphere.

Determination of the value of the business you are selling can be one of the most challenging aspects of a one-time sale. In theory, the agent taking on your business stands to earn at least what you have earned each year, with perhaps some moderate initial devaluation with you no longer at the helm. However, the more systems, processes, and infrastructure you have in place, the more likely your business is to be able to keep running even as you cleanly step away. The more capable and talented the new farmer, the greater his or her potential for long-term income. Generally, a business is valued at about three times its annual net income at the time of sale. So, if your business nets $100,000 a year, you might consider selling for $300,000.

When planned wisely, a one-time sale can be a sound option, allowing a retiring rainmaker to completely step away from the business with a windfall payout that, invested and managed wisely, can provide a substantial retirement nest egg. Keep in mind that the one-time sale, unless paid in cash, carries the same risks of potential default of any financed sale, so be certain the buyer is well-qualified and capable of paying back a note or any other instrument used to finance the purchase.

The referral-based phased sale

This second method of selling your farm requires a longer-term investment of time and effort on the part of the rainmaker, but has the potential of yielding greater long-term rewards. In the referral-based phased-sale method, the rainmaker trains and mentors the new agent to conduct the business as similarly as possible to the business the rainmaker has established. The rainmaker gradually introduces the incoming agent to his or her past clients, sphere of influence, and other agents with whom he or she has built relationships. The incoming agent begins to work with and oversee support staff and team members.

The rainmaker and the incoming agent initially attend buyer appointments and listing interviews together, gradually transitioning the business as the incoming agent takes on greater responsibility over time. Once the rainmaker feels the agent taking on the business is almost interchangeable with the rainmaker in the eyes of their clientele, team, and staff, the rainmaker begins to step away, allowing the agent to become more and more independent.

Though the rainmaker may eventually be able relocate away from the farm area, in this model it is vital that they continue to maintain the relationships they have established over the years. The rainmaker should commit to calling or checking in with their past clients and sphere with diminishing frequency over a period of at least five years. If relocating, the rainmaker may need to return to the farm area periodically for community or client appreciation events they once sponsored.

The rainmaker should also commit to keeping his or her cell number, website, and social media accounts active for a predetermined period of time, to continue to answer phone calls, emails, texts, and other inquiries that might continue to come their way as they exit the business, and to promptly pass leads or inquiries along to the incoming agent. The greater the exiting rainmaker's visibility, responsiveness, and involvement, the more repeat and referral business will flow to the new agent.

The referral structure used in this model follows a diminishing structure over a period of years whereby the rainmaker continues to earn referral income as the new agent takes on the full responsibilities of the business. Gradually, the rainmaker will transition out of the business as fewer inquiries come their way and as their level of visibility and involvement in the farm area decreases. The graduated split generally looks something like this:

- Year 1: 50/50

- Year 2: 60 incoming agent/40 exiting rainmaker

- Year 3: 70 incoming agent/30 exiting rainmaker

- Year 4: 80 incoming agent/20 exiting rainmaker

- Year 5: 90 incoming agent/10 exiting rainmaker

In the previous example, by year six the exiting rainmaker has completely retired and is no longer responsible for any involvement in the farm area or follow-up with leads, past clients, or sphere. If the outgoing rainmaker is planning a quicker exit, this structure might be more aggressive while a longer-term exit might make the structure more gradual.

Some agreements also allow for referral exceptions where a lead and resulting transaction is solely the result of the incoming agent's sphere or efforts, while other agreements include a blanket referral for all closed transactions regardless of the source of business. Some agreements include a permanent per-transaction referral fee for those few and far between leads that may come through the exiting rainmaker. However, for most exiting rainmakers, the time and expense associated with keeping a license in referral status long-term are not worth the relatively small referral income.

INTERVIEW WITH A FAMOUS FARMER
ANGIE TALLANT

Angie Tallant is the award-winning owner of Somers & Associates in Fairbanks, Alaska. She joined S&A while the company was in its early stages of growth and went on to take over the business and the brokerage and then to expand the brokerage into several top-producing locations. Here, Angie shares how she achieved her success.

continued

How did your career in real estate begin?

I was originally hired at Somers & Associates as the office manager, basically an administrative position. Eventually I became the assistant to the broker and decided to get my real estate license. I worked as the broker's assistant for 11 years, during which time I learned every aspect of the business.

How did your relationship with your broker evolve?

After my third year, I fell in love with the industry, working with people, and making a difference in their lives. I told my broker all the time that I was going to buy the business from him one day. My broker became more and more active with The National Association of Realtors, which caused him to be absent more often. During times he was away, I stepped in to take over his duties. Eventually, we became interchangeable. When my broker decided to move to Mexico, he agreed to sell me the business.

What were the most valuable lessons your learned from the outgoing broker?

He always treated his agents as though they were his clients. He also taught me that the priority is never about quantity, but about having a culture within the office. Learning to say no to people when they do not appear to be a good fit is also important.

Did you face any challenges as you took over the business?

The biggest challenge was keeping the established brand in place while repositioning to meet the needs of a new generation. We had a great foundation but some pieces were missing on the tech side. I rebranded, keeping new generations of clients in mind. I didn't have any formal training, so I worked every role in the company to learn and understand it. I created a marketing plan and reached out to other agents to share my approach. After eight months I had 13 agents from other brokerages come over to join my office. I eventually bought out another brokerage and purchased that office, making that the North Pole branch, then opened our third office by recruiting people I knew.

How was your business transfer structured?

My broker stayed on for three years as I learned to run all aspects of the brokerage and made technology upgrades. We paid referrals back and forth on a case-by-case basis as appropriate. Since we had complete trust, we always made sure it was all fair, but we also put a written agreement in place.

continued

Did the outgoing agent remain involved in the business in any manner?

Yes, in fact my broker and his wife now work for me. My broker's son also joined us and took over my old role. We built a large foreclosure business, which they still run. My broker now winters in Mexico and returns to Alaska in the summer.

Looking back, is there anything you would have done differently?

One thing I've learned in business is that you can't be afraid to take risks. Sometimes you fail and it's okay to fail. Following that philosophy has helped me grow my brokerage to the largest in town, with over 25% market share. We have now expanded to 65 agents with three branch offices.

WHAT'S NEXT?

WE HOPE YOU have found this book to be a wealth of information, inspiration, and new ideas for taking your business to the next level through real estate farming. Now that you have all of the tools and knowledge you need to sow the seeds, harvest the crops, and reap the rewards of a successful real estate farm, we'd love to hear from you. Share your success stories, which tools and systems are working for you, and feedback about Farming, for Real Estate Agents at realestaterainmakers.com; on Instagram at farmingforrealestateagents; or on Facebook at Farming, for Real Estate Agents.

For ready-to-use worksheets, workbook tracking forms, and more system resources, download the Famous Agent Systems app.

We also offer coaching. Sign up to access the success systems outlined in this book and to discover how accountability can help your business grow by visiting realestaterainmakers.com.

Wishing you fruitful farming and real estate fame!

ACKNOWLEDGMENTS

CASEY KASEM IS quoted as saying, "Success doesn't happen in a vacuum. You're only as good as the people you work with and the people you work for."

In real estate this is especially true. I would be remiss in failing to thank the many people who have helped to make my business a success and have given me the freedom to write this book. My original mentor, Judy Howlin, to whom this book is dedicated, gifted me with the foundation of exceptional mentorship and the wings of trust and confidence, for which I will be forever grateful.

I would not be where I am today without the partnership of my very first team member, Valerie Harnois, still my business partner today (and now my podcast sidekick). She has gamely stayed by my side through many evolutions of my business and has made my occasional growing pains much more tolerable with her fabulous sense of humor, her fiery spirit, and her unwavering friendship.

I am also immensely grateful for the trust and partnership of my broker, Chris McMahon, who entrusted me to grow his brokerage brand, Old Line Properties, by opening its first branch office. Chris's patience, sound counsel, and steadfast leadership have allowed me to take my business to new heights.

Thank you to my incredible team—I am privileged to be in business with each of you. Your growth and success are my constant joy.

I am also so very grateful for my farm, the Kentlands neighborhood, which has given me so much, including the best place on earth to raise my children, a community of the most wonderful friends I could imagine, and immeasurable rewards I work daily to reciprocate.

Last, but by no means least, my eternal and greatest thanks goes to my wonderful family: my parents, who instilled in me the belief that I could do anything; my siblings, who have been my cheerleaders and who are some of my dearest friends; my children, who embrace me with their love and understanding despite the many hours I devote to my business and my creative outlets; and my wonderful husband, Chris, whose unconditional love and support have been my fuel, my freedom, and my solace.

ABOUT THE AUTHOR

MEREDITH FOGLE, known as Kentlands' resident realtor, is a top-producing real estate agent and team leader in one of the most sought-after areas of the Washington, DC, suburbs.

A life-long resident of the Washington, DC, area, Meredith has been licensed in real estate since 1998. She harnessed the power of real estate farming to launch an award-winning career, achieving Founders Club (the highest level of achievement) status during her years with her first brokerage, Long and Foster; membership in Remax's prestigious Hall of Fame; and has been awarded year after year as a top agent in her area. Meredith opened a bespoke branch office for Old Line Properties in 2014. Most recently, she was recognized as one of the top 250 agents by volume by *DC Metro Area Real Producers* magazine. Meredith is widely known as the Kentlands real estate expert.

Meredith attended Stone Ridge School in Bethesda, MD, and is a summa cum laude graduate of the Catholic University of America in Washington, DC. She holds the National

Association of Realtors' esteemed CRS, e-Pro, and PSA designations, and is a member of the invitation-only Top Agent Network. Meredith has been a keynote speaker for the Greater Capital Area Association of Realtors, sits on several local boards, holds the business seat for and serves as Vice Chair of the Kentlands Community Foundation, and serves as executive producer and founder of Kentlands Community Players theatre company.

A frequent contributor to local newspapers and television programs (most recently, *Good Morning Washington* and the *Washington Post*), Meredith is also a published author and frequent real estate blogger. Meredith has developed the popular real estate training program "Career Kick Start," and serves as a mentor and real estate coach. She is also the host of the popular real estate podcast, *So You Want to Be a Real Estate Agent*. Meredith lives in the Kentlands with her husband, her three children, and her mother.